Black Sea

Tabríz

Sulaymáníyyah Qazvín Badasht

Ṭihrán

Euphrates River

'Akká
Haifa

Baghdád

Tigris River

Yazd

Persian Gulf

Shíráz

The Central Figures

Bahá'u'lláh

Volume One

Other Books in the Central Figures Series
Compiled by the National Bahá'í Education Task Force:

The Central Figures: Bahá'u'lláh, Volumes 2, 3
The Central Figures: The Báb, Volumes 1, 2, 3
The Central Figures: 'Abdu'l-Bahá, Volumes 1, 2, 3

For more information about
forthcoming works in this series,
the scope and sequence of the
Core Curriculum for Spiritual Education,
and training programs for teachers and parents,
please contact:
    National Teacher Training Center
    Louhelen Bahá'í School
    3208 South State Road
    Davison, Michigan 48423
    email nttc@usbnc.org
    telephone 810-653-5033

The Central Figures

Bahá'u'lláh

Volume One

Core Curriculum for Spiritual Education · Stories
National Spiritual Assembly of the Bahá'ís of the United States

Bahá'í Publishing Trust
Wilmette, Illinois

Graphic Design by Pepper Peterson Oldziey

Bahá'í Publishing Trust, Wilmette, Illinois 60091-2886
Copyright © 2001 by the National Spiritual Assembly
of the Bahá'ís of the United States of America
All rights reserved
Published 2001
04 03 02 01   4 3 2 1

Printed in the United States of America

Illustrations: cover © 2001 David S. Ruhe; pp. 1–16 © 2001 Carla Trimble; pp. 47–62 © 2001 Winifred Barnum-Newman; pp. 63–76 © 2001 Cindy Pacileo; pp. 94, 100–102 © 2001 Carrie Kneisler. All other illustrations © 2001 National Spiritual Assembly of the Bahá'ís of the United States.

Dedicated with love to

*Hand of the Cause of God
Amatu'l-Bahá Rúḥíyyih Khánum*

Contents

Foreword — ix

Preface — x

1. Prayers and Meditations of Bahá'u'lláh — 1
Saving the Silver-Tongued Nightingale — 3
A Prayer for Mírzá Ja'far — 8
The Tree of Life — 11

2. Loving Acts of Bahá'u'lláh — 17
Father of the Poor — 19
One Meritorious Act — 22
The Friend at the Crossroads — 27

3. Bahá'u'lláh and the Children of His Household — 31
Summertime — 33
The Prison and the Garden — 38
The Power of Love — 41

4. The Station of Bahá'u'lláh as Stated by 'Abdu'l-Bahá — 47
The Prisoner with Power — 49
The Truth of Bahá'u'lláh's Mission — 54
The Greatest Father-Son Story of All Time — 57

5. The Childhood of Bahá'u'lláh — 63
Bahá'u'lláh's Fishes — 65
Bahá'u'lláh Is Born — 70
The Puppet Show — 73

77	**6**	**The Youth and Early Manhood of Bahá'u'lláh**
79		The Badasht Conference
84		Lives of Service
87		Escape to Ṭihrán
93	**7**	**Principles Related to the Oneness of God and the Oneness of Humanity**
95		Isfandíyár
100		A Journey across a Desert
103		Thank You, Isfandíyár
109		Appendix: Questions for Reflection and Discussion
112		Glossary
115		Bibliography
117		Index

Foreword

July 2001

Dear Bahá'í Children,

You are the most precious treasure in our community. We want you to grow strong and to be happy. When you grow up, you will become leaders in the Bahá'í community.

The most important way to begin your Bahá'í education is to learn about the life and teachings of Bahá'u'lláh (The Glory of God). Bahá'u'lláh's Teachings bring God's love to people of all religions, nations, and races. When you learn about Bahá'u'lláh's life, you will see how He helped people and changed their hearts, and you will grow to love and admire Him. From His example, you will also learn how to help people improve their lives and be happy. And you will learn how to improve your own life.

Learning about Bahá'u'lláh will help you understand the power of prayer, the importance of service and sacrifice, and the powers of courage and love. We hope that, through the stories in this book, you will learn how to bring His Teachings into action in your own life.

You are always in our hearts and in our prayers,

Robert C. Henderson
Secretary-General
National Spiritual Assembly of the
Bahá'ís of the United States

Preface

These stories offer a glimpse of the majestic life of Bahá'u'lláh, His world-embracing teachings, and the effect of His life and teachings upon the lives of His countless followers everywhere. The stories are written to appeal to young and old and to be used in homes, schools, and informal gatherings of the friends. They are the first in a comprehensive series of books designed to draw the heart to the love of God and humanity and to inspire expression of that love in service.

Because the stories are aligned with the goals and topics of the Core Curriculum for Spiritual Education, a comprehensive spiritual education program of the National Spiritual Assembly of the Bahá'ís of the United States, they may be readily incorporated into a system of classroom learning. They may also be enjoyed in a family setting.

Short quotations are included with the stories for memorization or reflection. These quotations express fundamental spiritual principles that the stories illustrate. The shortest stories appeal to the youngest readers. The longer stories build understanding for older children and junior youth. The book includes a glossary, map, and discussion questions to extend the learning possibilities for individuals of all ages. Lesson plans to accompany the stories, published as *Core Curriculum Learning Activities: Bahá'u'lláh*, may be ordered through the U.S. Bahá'í Distribution Service at 4703 Fulton Industrial Boulevard, Atlanta, Georgia 30336-2017, or by telephone at 1-800-999-9019.

This first Core Curriculum storybook represents a gift of love from artists, illustrators, and editors. The National Bahá'í Education Task Force particularly acknowledges a debt of gratitude for the assistance of Susanne Alexander, Iraj Ayman, Mary Firdawsi, Sherveen Lotfi, Catherine Vance, and many others. Dr. David Ruhe contributed the cover art.

The book responds to the call of the beloved Universal House of Justice for an increase of attention to the spiritual and practical education of children everywhere.

— National Bahá'í Education Task Force

Prayers and Meditations of Bahá'u'lláh

1

Make my prayer, O my Lord,
a fountain of living waters
whereby I may live
as long as Thy sovereignty
endureth, and may
make mention of Thee
in every world of Thy worlds.

— Bahá'u'lláh, *The Kitáb-i-Aqdas*, p. 93

Saving the Silver-Tongued Nightingale

Written by Jean Gould
Illustrated by Carla Trimble

One day, late in the 19th century, a child was born in Yazd in the ancient land of Persia. He was given the name 'Alí-Muḥammad. He grew up to become a learned man and a talented poet and thus earned the right to be called Mírzá 'Alí-Muḥammad. Eventually, Bahá'u'lláh declared that he had earned an additional name: "Varqá," which means "Nightingale."

As a poet and a writer, Mírzá 'Alí-Muḥammad Varqá certainly lived up to his name. In fact, the Hand of the Cause of God H. M. Balyuzi later referred to him as the Silver-Tongued Nightingale. In addition, he also had an exceptional knowledge of medicine, the Muslim scriptures, and the history and literature of his country. Is it any wonder that the Crown Prince of Persia

Bahá'u'lláh: Prayers and Meditations of Bahá'u'lláh

himself would often call for Varqá to sit in an assemblage of learned men so that he might charm and delight them with the music of his words?

Varqá, however, had a mother-in-law who was neither charmed nor delighted by his words. She was a devout Muslim lady of the S̲h̲áhsavan tribe, and she believed the lies the enemies of the Bahá'í Faith were telling about the Bahá'í believers in Persia. As well, along with most of her fellow Muslims at that time, she believed in her heart that Muḥammad was the last and final Messenger from God. She knew that Bahá'u'lláh claimed to be a new Messenger from God for this day. In her mind, this was an outrageous claim. Feeling no need to investigate the truth for herself, she simply declared Bahá'u'lláh an enemy. Of course, she also declared as an enemy any Muslim who left his faith and gave allegiance to Bahá'u'lláh.

Varqá was one of these. At an early age, he had recognized Bahá'u'lláh's station as the King of Kings. And with his silver tongue, he had been singing His praises ever since.

Such poems, such beautiful words, should win over any heart, but the S̲h̲áhsavan lady would not listen nor be convinced. Finally, only hatred for her son-in-law seethed in her heart, and she decided she must put a stop to his words, the words that were bringing such shame to their family circle. Soon it became clear to her that only death could still Varqá forever, and so she plotted to have him killed.

Bahá'u'lláh: Prayers and Meditations of Bahá'u'lláh

First she told a servant of the house that he would get a fine horse and a lot of money if he would do the job. Unbeknownst to his employer, however, the servant had also joined the ranks of Bahá'u'lláh's followers. Naturally, he warned his fellow Bahá'í to go into hiding.

Realizing he must turn his back on his home, Varqá planned his escape. In the dead of night, he dropped his precious papers and other belongings from a window to the black street below. Then he crept quietly from the dark sleeping house, gathered up his things, and stole silently away into the dark, beyond the reach of his determined mother-in-law.

When she learned of the escape, his enemy was enraged. One of her relatives was a mujtahid, a doctor of Islamic law, a person of high authority. Surely he would help. Surely he could issue the official death warrant she coveted.

"My son-in-law is a Bábí*," she shouted. "He ought to be put to death."

Unfortunately for the Sháhsavan lady, her relative was a just man. He knew nothing of the case, he said. There was nothing he could do. She must have proof if she wanted to make her case.

Fortunately for the Sháhsavan lady, Varqá had a certain son named Rúḥu'lláh. Rúḥu'lláh had been with his father when he had attained the presence of Baha'u'lláh for the second time. Rúḥu'lláh was only seven then, but he had recognized the station of the King of Glory. He knew. "O the joy of that day," he said later.

Fortunately for the Sháhsavan lady as well, Rúḥu'lláh had his father's gift for poetry and clear speaking. She believed he would do very nicely for proof. On that day, Rúḥu'lláh followed his angry grandmother into the presence of the mujtahid. "I will prove to you through this child the apostasy of my son-in-law," she declared triumphantly. Could he know the meaning of such a word? Maybe not, but he certainly knew what to do when the mujtahid, that good man, asked whether Rúḥu'lláh could say his daily prayer.

* In the late nineteenth century in Persia, many people still referred to Bahá'ís as Bábís.

First there was the obligation of ablution, the washing of hands and face to prepare himself to meet his Lord in prayer. Then he turned to face the Holy Land where Bahá'u'lláh was imprisoned. He said Bahá'u'lláh's Long Obligatory Prayer. Like his father's, his voice was sweet and beautiful.

After a moment, it was the mujtahid's turn to speak. What kind of man, he said, could raise such a wonderful child? His condemnation, his death, would be a terrible thing. Her deed, her wish, was horrid and unforgivable.

She returned home shame-faced and disappointed, while the prayer of a child became a father's salvation. Mírzá 'Alí-Muḥammad Varqá, the Silver-Tongued Nightingale, had, for the moment, been set free. ★

Bahá'u'lláh: Prayers and Meditations of Bahá'u'lláh

A Prayer for Mírzá Ja'far

Written by Gail Radley
Photography by Pepper Oldziey

The August sun burned down on the stone walls of 'Akká as the sailboat rocked roughly into the harbor. The Bahá'ís had come a long way. They were hot, hungry, and thirsty. But Mírzá Ja'far was happy—he was with Bahá'u'lláh!

The townspeople yelled at them from the streets, from windows and doorways, as they passed. Mírzá Ja'far had walked through hateful mobs before. He had been hungry, tired, and hot before. These things did not matter. He was happy.

The guards at the mighty stone prison gave them little to eat and drink. But Mírzá Ja'far thanked God. His dark, narrow cell seemed like a sweet-smelling rose garden with Bahá'u'lláh close by.

Then, one day, Mírzá Ja'far fell sick. How could it be? They had crossed deserts and climbed mountains together. Eager always to help, Mírzá Ja'far never complained, and he never seemed to need rest. He was the one who went with 'Abdu'l-Bahá to find supplies while others rested.

Now Mírzá Ja'far grew more and more sick. The doctor turned away. He knew of nothing that would help his patient. Mírzá Ja'far drew in his last breath.

Bahá'u'lláh's secretary rushed to tell Bahá'u'lláh that their beloved Mírzá Ja'far was dead.

"Chant the prayer . . . O Thou, the Healer," said Bahá'u'lláh, "and Mírzá Ja'far will come alive."

Quickly, the Bahá'ís obeyed. Soon Mírzá Ja'far's lifeless body grew warm. Next he began to move. Then he sat up, laughing and joking with his friends.

"Praise be to God!" Mírzá Ja'far cried. He would live to serve Bahá'u'lláh for a long time to come! ★

Retold from a story by 'Abdu'l-Bahá, *Memorials of the Faithful*, pp. 156–58

Intone, O My servant, the verses of God
that have been received by thee,
as intoned by them who have
drawn nigh unto Him,
that the sweetness of thy melody
may kindle thine own soul,
and attract the hearts of all men.
Whoso reciteth, in the
privacy of his chamber,
the verses revealed by God,
the scattering angels of the Almighty
shall scatter abroad the fragrance
of the words uttered by his mouth,
and shall cause the heart
of every righteous man to throb.

— Bahá'u'lláh, *Gleanings from the Writings of Bahá'u'lláh*, p. 295

The Tree of Life

Written by Rick Johnson   Illustrated by Carla Trimble

  I love the long walks Grandma and I take every day when I visit her in the summer. Today, we're walking out to where Grandpa is mowing hay in the meadow. As we walk, we see the tractor going back and forth in the distance. My sister, Lua, is riding with him. Grandma and I like to share our work, so, between us, we carry a basket that contains some donuts we've made, some apples, and a big glass jar filled with ice water.

  Across the prairie we see Grandpa and Lua waving to us. The tractor stops under a big cottonwood tree that offers the only shady spot. They wait for us there.

  The huge cottonwood, as wide as several people, is the only tree one can see that is not along a stream or near a house. It's one of my favorite places on Grandma and Grandpa's farm, and I come here often. Grandma even calls it "Carol's Tree." It's a place that gives me a special feeling of peace that I treasure.

Bahá'u'lláh: Prayers and Meditations of Bahá'u'lláh

After everyone gets hellos and hugs all around, I spread out a cloth for us to sit on, and Grandma sets out the donuts. Lua slices the apples.

My summer visit is almost over. Next year I go to college, and I've been thinking a lot about how things change and what's important to me. I've got something I've been thinking about, and I want to tell about it.

"Grandma," I begin, "why do you think this tree grew alone by itself like this?" It was something I'd pondered many times as I sat under it, watching the sun set over the hills—another of my favorite things about Grandma's place.

"Well, I imagine it probably had something to do with weather and the soil and . . . ."

"No, Grandma," I giggle. "Can't you see that it's not alone?" Grandma's gentle smile shows she's curious—she knows I'm up to something! We often make jokes with one another like this, so she's not sure whether I'm serious or not. She munches on an apple slice and waits to see what happens.

"But Carol, the nearest other tree I see is at least a mile away," Lua protests. "That looks pretty obvious."

"That's just it, Lua, you've gotta look beyond the obvious!"

"Okay, so what's your point?" Lua says in confusion.

I grab one of the massive tree roots and pretend that I'm trying to pull it loose from the ground. "See, Lua, it's pretty connected—not off by itself at all!"

"Oh, Carol," Lua snorts in disgust, "that's not what I mean!"

"Which is exactly my point, Lua. We look so much at what makes us seem separate that we miss the way everything is connected. That tree is no more alone than I'm a flying pig!"

"Carol, don't tempt me . . . " Lua snickers. Everyone laughs.

"Well, Carol, I can see you're getting to be quite the scientist," Grandpa comments.

"It's more than science, Grandpa." I grab the root again. "Do you remember that, each morning, Bahá'u'lláh chanted prayers with His family and told them stories about the Prophets? That's exactly like this tree sinking its roots into the good black earth. Praying together sustains the family, just as the earth sustains the tree."

"Land sakes, Carol, how did you come up with that?" Grandpa looks at me with serious interest.

"Well, when I visit, I like to come out here every day at sunset. It's like recharging my batteries from all the stuff that happens. I bring my prayer book and just sit here and think and pray and watch the sunset. It's so beautiful and it really gets me thinking. . . ."

"I realize how much I depend on my family—and praying with them. When we pray, it pulls us together and connects us with the Divine Power that sustains everything. When we say prayers together before school and work, I can't see those prayers. But it's like the tiny roots that we can't see that connect this tree with the earth. All our 'little' prayers are like a big web of roots that hold a family together when the going gets tough."

Bahá'u'lláh: Prayers and Meditations of Bahá'u'lláh

"I guess that's why this tree has been able to stand here through all the storms, blizzards, and droughts," Grandma remarks. "It doesn't seem to mind all the changes in weather."

"Roots growing deep in the earth can always find water and have something solid to hold onto," Grandpa observes. "We can pull on that root all day, and it won't budge!"

"When I think of all the suffering that Bahá'u'lláh and His family endured," I add, "it just seems so clear that, because they prayed together, they could find the 'water of life' and have something solid to hold onto."

"I guess there's no such thing as being completely alone, is there?" Grandma says, taking my hand and squeezing it.

"We look alone, but really, everything is connected. The tree 'knows' that's true without even having to think about it," I reply.

"But we can fool ourselves, can't we?" Lua asks.

"That's part of it," I respond, "but I've got another question—How are roots and leaves alike?"

Lua lets her eyes follow the sturdy trunk up into the graceful, curving branches and delicate leaves. "Well, they're part of the tree...."

"And they've gotta have each other, Lua! Just like in a family, the roots die without the leaves, and the leaves die without the roots."

Grandma gives me a wonderful look of love and respect. I love the way she listens to me.

"In a family, prayer is the root and love is the branch," Grandma says. "Because I love you and you love me, I want more than anything to be kind to you. Kindness just feels like the right thing when there's real love. In Bahá'u'lláh's family, courtesy and kindness were so natural that everyone acted that way without thinking about it—it was almost born into them."

"Like the trunk is 'born into' the tree," I laugh. "Respect and courtesy were natural in Bahá'u'lláh's family, because good manners were the 'trunk' of the family—strong roots make the trunk strong. Like in the tree, you don't have to force people to respect each other if they do it day by day."

Grandpa puts his arm around me and I hug him tightly. He smells of sweet new-mown hay. "Grandpa, when I hear that wonderful rustling of leaves overhead, do you know what I think?"

"No, Carol, what?"

"I think that I know why 'Abdu'l-Bahá and Bahíyyih Khánum are known as the Most Great Branch and the Greatest Holy Leaf!"

Grandma smiles and offers me a drink. My eyes fill with tears. "Oh, Grandma, I can't express it, but I just keep thinking of how much the children loved Bahá'u'lláh and how He took an interest in everything that concerned them, even the littlest things. You and Grandpa make me feel that way, too!"

"It's as you said," Grandma replies, pulling me close and pressing me to her heart. "Everything is connected to everything else. Bahá'u'lláh loved and trained His children; 'Abdu'l-Bahá and Bahíyyih K͟hánum loved and trained the Guardian; the Guardian loved and trained me when I was on Pilgrimage; I did my best to love and train your mother, and she and your father are doing their best to love and train you. If you see that the result is good, remember the tiny hidden roots where everything reaches the Divine Water of Life. We're the trunk that grows from that. You taught us that today, Carol."

"Do you think that's why one of the titles of Bahá'u'lláh is the Tree of Life?" I ask.

"Yes, child, everything is a part of that Tree," Grandma whispers. ★

Bahá'u'lláh: Prayers and Meditations of Bahá'u'lláh

Loving Acts of Bahá'u'lláh

O SON OF MAN!
I loved thy creation,
hence I created thee.
Wherefore, do thou love Me,
that I may name thy name
and fill thy soul
with the spirit of life.

— **Bahá'u'lláh**, *Hidden Words*, Arabic No. 4

Father of the Poor

Written by Gail Radley
Illustrated by Jai Kenyatta-Anderson

    Before Mírzá Ḥusayn-'Alí was called Bahá'u'lláh, before He was known as the Promised One of God, He was called by another title: "Father of the Poor." Mírzá Ḥusayn-'Alí was born into a wealthy family. His father was a mírzá, a nobleman, who was so respected for his talents, wisdom, generosity, and courage that the Sháh gave him the title "Buzurg," meaning "the great one," and made him governor.

    Mírzá Buzurg owned a vast estate, and many peasants worked the land and tended his livestock for him. Often young Mírzá Ḥusayn-'Alí walked or rode His horse through the countryside, stopping to speak with the peasants and learn about their lives and troubles. Believing that He would one day rule the estate, the peasants watched Him as He grew and were no doubt comforted by the understanding Mírzá Ḥusayn-'Alí showed.

When He was nearly eighteen, Mírzá Ḥusayn-'Alí married Ásíyih Khánum, the daughter of another wealthy nobleman. Ásíyih Khánum had everything a young woman in Persia could hope to have. She was tall and beautiful, wise, gentle, and kind. The young couple started their life together with great wealth and comfort. A jeweler worked for six months fashioning her jewels, even creating gold buttons studded with gems for her clothing. Forty mules carried Ásíyih Khánum's belongings to her new home. The couple would, everyone thought, enjoy a grand life of power and luxury, filled with parties and important ceremonies.

But Mírzá Ḥusayn-'Alí was not interested in living a life of wealth and ease. He had never forgotten the poor peasants whose lives had touched His heart, and so He was rarely seen among the wealthy and powerful. Instead, He and Ásíyih Khánum took care of the poor. They listened to their problems and tried to help them. Often they invited them to share meals with them. No needy person was ever turned away. Because of the kind comfort she offered so willingly, Ásíyih Khánum soon earned the title "Mother of Consolation." And the generous, wise Mírzá Ḥusayn-'Alí was known as "Father of the Poor."

It was no wonder that Mírzá Ḥusayn-'Alí and Ásíyih Khánum's children would grow to have the same loving and generous hearts.

One day, their Son 'Abdu'l-Bahá set off to see His Father's sheep, just as His Father had done as a young Man. What a sight it must have been—thousands of them roamed the mountainsides! The shepherds were happy to be visited by their kind, young master, and they prepared a feast for Him.

Finally, it was time for 'Abdu'l-Bahá to go home.

The head shepherd drew 'Abdu'l-Bahá aside. "It is the custom to leave the shepherds a gift," the shepherd told him.

"But I have nothing to give," 'Abdu'l-Bahá replied.

"They have just given you a feast," the shepherd pointed out. "You must give them something."

'Abdu'l-Bahá thought a moment and then decided. "I will give them all the sheep!"

'Abdu'l-Bahá must have wondered what His Father would say when He learned that His Son had given away thousands of His sheep.

But Mírzá Ḥusayn-'Alí only laughed. "We will have to protect 'Abdu'l-Bahá from Himself," He said. "Some day He will give Himself away!"

Bahá'u'lláh truly was the "Father of the Poor." ★

One Meritorious Act

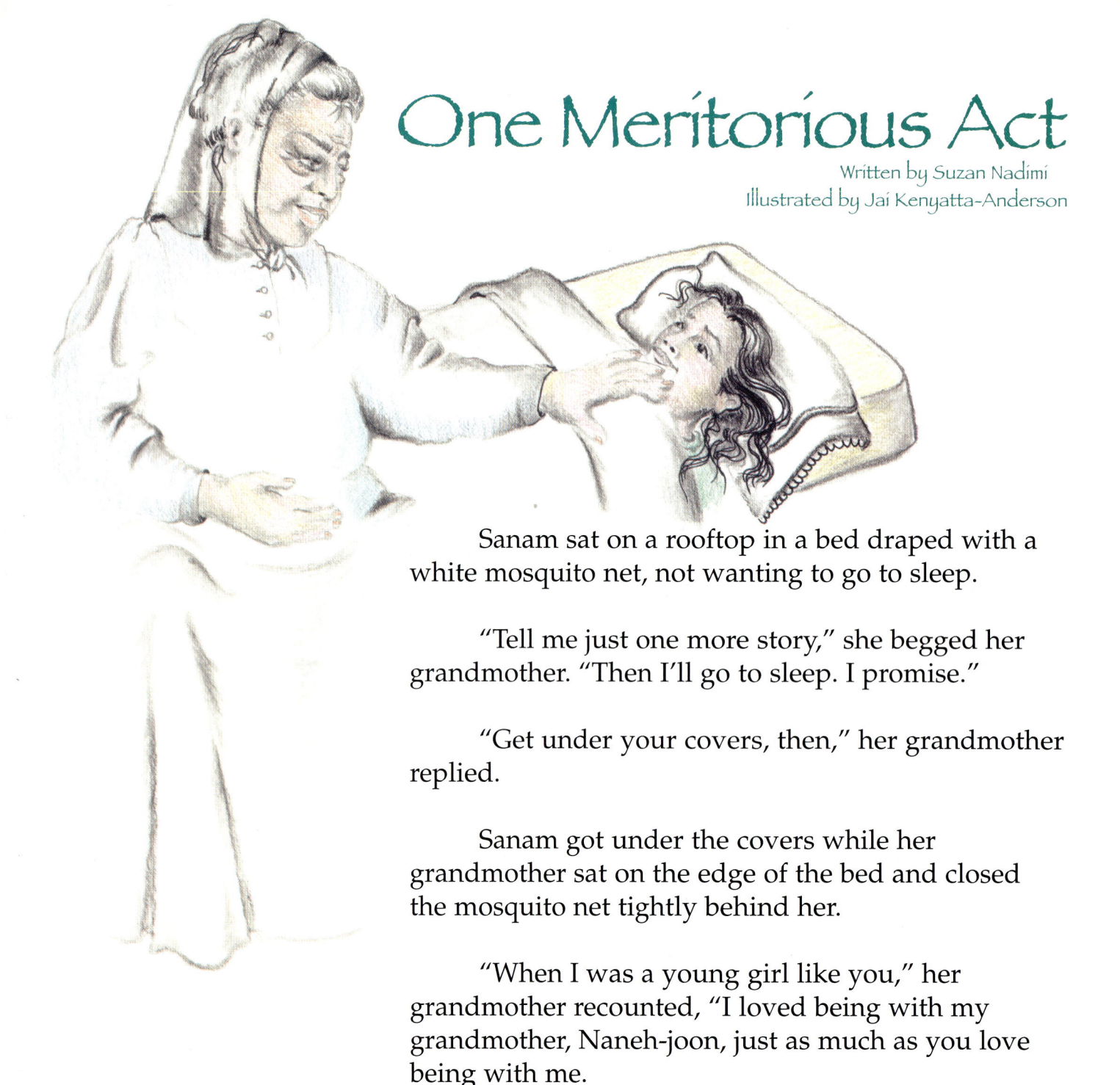

Written by Suzan Nadimi
Illustrated by Jai Kenyatta-Anderson

Sanam sat on a rooftop in a bed draped with a white mosquito net, not wanting to go to sleep.

"Tell me just one more story," she begged her grandmother. "Then I'll go to sleep. I promise."

"Get under your covers, then," her grandmother replied.

Sanam got under the covers while her grandmother sat on the edge of the bed and closed the mosquito net tightly behind her.

"When I was a young girl like you," her grandmother recounted, "I loved being with my grandmother, Naneh-joon, just as much as you love being with me.

"Naneh-joon was a very devout Muslim. She got up to pray before the sun rose and went to bed after her midnight prayer. Even in her old age and poor health, she went to the mosque every day. She gave money to the poor and was kind to all.

"One hot day in August, Naneh-joon gave me permission to accompany her on her daily journey to the mosque.

" 'On the occasion of your turning nine,' she said, 'you may come with me to the mosque. But you must cover yourself well and be silent as a mouse in God's house.'

"I held my chador tightly in place under my chin with one hand, and with the other I held Naneh-joon's. We went through the alleys of southern Tiḥrán. I was going to the mosque!

"As we drew near to the mosque, we heard loud noises echoing between the clay houses.

" 'Bábí! Bábí!' The sound of people shouting reached our ears. 'Enemy of Islám!'

"Naneh-joon gripped my hand. 'Those Bábís!' she hissed. 'The mullá says they are bad people. They do things I shudder to tell you.'

"I wanted to free my hand from Naneh-joon's tight grasp. 'Please, Naneh-joon,' I pleaded. 'Let's go home.' I wanted my Naneh-joon back, not this stranger with an angry look in her eyes.

" 'The mullá says that hurting any Bábí helps the Prophet Muḥammad,' Naneh-joon said.

"Naneh-joon pulled me toward the noise, walking faster than I had ever seen her. She pushed and shoved until we were at the front of the crowd that was shouting and throwing stones.

"Then and there was the first and last time I saw Him. He was barefooted and bareheaded, but I felt I was standing in the presence of the King of Kings. I stood mesmerized, shutting out the noise of the people and seeing nothing but the glory surrounding Him.

"Naneh-joon let go of my hand, and I jolted out of my trance. I saw her picking up a stone.

" 'No!' I shouted. But she did not listen to me. She was about to step forward when an old woman ran ahead of her into the street.

"The old woman's frame shook with rage as she stepped forward and raised her hand to throw her stone at Him.

" 'By the Holy Imám, I beg you,' the old woman pleaded with the guards surrounding Him. 'Give me a chance to fling my stone in His face!'

"The King of Kings turned to His guards and said, 'Suffer not this woman to be disappointed. Deny her not what she regards as a meritorious act in the sight of God.'

"Tears welled up in my eyes at the words that had passed through His lips. I looked up and saw, through my tears, my old Naneh-joon standing by my side. She had dropped her stone to the ground. She took hold of my hand, and we walked back to her house in silence."

"Then what happened?" asked Sanam.

"I'm not going to tell you the story of how Naneh-joon and I became Bahá'ís, Sanam!" her grandmother said. "It is your bedtime!"

"Okay, okay!" replied Sanam.

Sanam made herself snug under the blankets. She prayed in her heart for Bahá'u'lláh to forgive the old woman for what she had done. Then she went to sleep. ★

Be generous in prosperity,
and thankful in adversity.
Be worthy of the trust of thy neighbor,
and look upon him with a bright
and friendly face.
Be a treasure to the poor,
an admonisher to the rich,
an answerer of the cry of the needy,
a preserver of the sanctity
of thy pledge.

— **Bahá'u'lláh,** *Gleanings from the Writings of Bahá'u'lláh,* p. 285

The Friend at the Crossroads

Written by Sally Cordova
Illustrated by Jai Kenyatta-Anderson

" 'How long have you been hungry?' He said that to me, Maryam. He didn't know me, but He knew I was hungry—hungry for many things. Why should He care?" marveled the old woman. "But He did."

The woman sat with her friend on a bench in the small dusty alley that she walked each day. She walked that alley in the hope of finding a reason to be going out. It was hard to stay indoors by herself. Her husband was long dead, as were most of the children they had had together. There was nothing to be done about it, no way to stop the sicknesses that came with each season and took so many away. The old woman often wondered why she had been spared. It seemed such a useless life with no one left to care for. Her daughters who still lived had gone with their husbands to another city, looking for a better life. They had asked her to come with them, but she was too old to go looking for better things. What could be out there for a poor woman of Baghdád?

Bahá'u'lláh: Loving Acts of Bahá'u'lláh

Maryam, her friend, was almost as old as she was. When they were feeling well enough, they often sat on this bench and tried to find something new to talk about.

"Oh, Maryam, I saw Him approaching me from a great distance. Well, at least as great a distance as these old eyes can see. He walked like a king, but kings don't come to this neighborhood!"

The two women had to laugh when they thought of that. Imagine a king getting his shoes dirty in their miserable part of the city! They stopped and regarded each other. It had been a long time since either one of them had found something to laugh about. Then they laughed again!

"Well," said the old woman, "before I could stop myself, I bent to kiss His hand. 'No, no, Mother,' He said, as He helped me to stand straight again. Yes, He called me 'Mother,' and just for a moment, I saw my dear son, Hasan, in His eyes. Oh, that child! I thought he might outlive me. But never mind.

"I saw such tenderness in His eyes. It was as if He knew me and everything I've ever suffered. I wanted so to kiss Him, to give back just a little of the love He was showing me. He knew this. He bent over so I could kiss His cheeks, and He asked me, 'How long have you been hungry?' He gave me some money, and I knew I could eat today. But do you know, Maryam, when I was talking to Him, my belly was not talking to me!"

The two women laughed again.

The next day, the old woman awoke early. Something seemed different about this day. True, her stomach did not hurt. She had eaten a good dinner the night before. But it was something more. She looked around her little house. The same patched ceiling, the same crumbling walls barely keeping out the wind. Then she knew. The glow of her meeting with the kind king, which was how she thought of Him, was still keeping her warm in her drafty old room. Her arms and legs that, yesterday, had moved so slowly now seemed to be pulling her out of bed to meet this new day.

And this was to be the way she started all her days for many days to come. At first, she wondered—would He be there? And He was there, on the side of the road, on His way to somewhere else, but always with time to spare for her. There would be the coins that made sure she was no longer hungry. But, better, there would be something to tell Maryam.

"He listens to me, Maryam. He never seems to be in a hurry, but I know He must have so many important things to do. I tell Him all my troubles, but these He already seems to know. Best of all, He seems to love me. It is as if my dear son, Hasan, has been returned to me—but He is even more than that. He sees past my aching bones, my wrinkled face, my patched clothes," she said with a wry smile. "He treats me with dignity. He makes me feel that I am important to someone, and I love Him. Who would have thought that this life had anything left for me?"

The old woman's happy meetings with her kind benefactor, Who was, of course, Bahá'u'lláh, lasted until He left Baghdád for Constantinople. Before He departed, He arranged for a daily allowance to be given to her for the rest of her life.

"You see, Maryam, He had to leave, but He did not forget me. I have more than enough to eat, my roof is patched, and I don't worry what will happen to me anymore. All these things are good, but He was the best thing of all. He looked into my soul and saw who I really was—and what He saw was enough."

"Peace, Maryam." ★

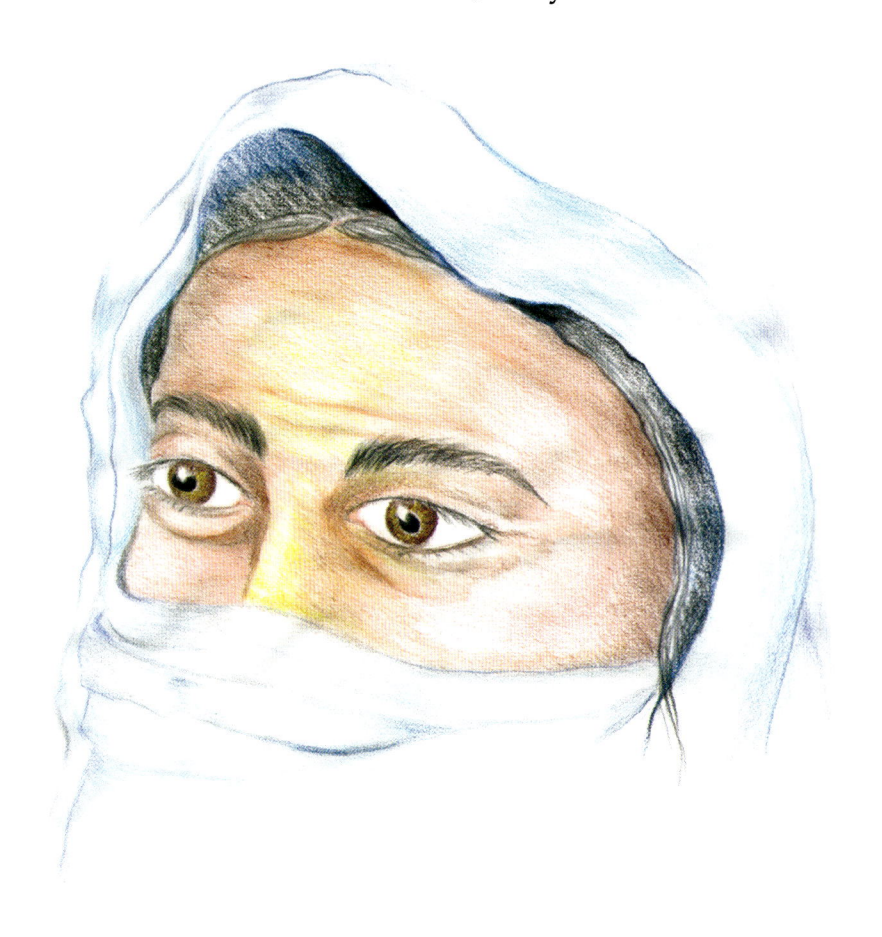

Bahá'u'lláh and the Children of His Household

O SON OF BEING!
Thy Paradise is My love;
thy heavenly home,
reunion with Me.
Enter therein and tarry not.
This is that which hath been
destined for thee
in Our kingdom above
and Our exalted Dominion.

— **Bahá'u'lláh,** *Hidden Words*, Arabic No. 6

Bahá'u'lláh: Bahá'u'lláh and the Children of His Household

Summertime

Written by Alexander Haskell
Illustrated by Nina Scott

The night was warm. Outside, the stars twinkled brightly, and the crickets were singing their nightly songs. Clara, lying in her darkened bedroom with a single sheet pulled up to her chin, waited expectantly for her mother.

"Why did God make it so hot in the summer and so cold in the winter? It's just too hot!"

"You're right, it does seem too hot, but just think about what you like in the summer."

"Well, playing with my friends, and swimming, and…."

Bahá'u'lláh: Bahá'u'lláh and the Children of His Household

"What about your favorite summertime fruits?"

"Like watermelon and grapes?"

"Yes, and the hotter the sun, the sweeter the fruits."

"Really?" said Clara.

"Really," said her mother. "What about this sheet covering you? Where did it come from?"

"The store?"

"Yes, dear, but I mean, what is it made of?"

"Colors and cotton?"

"Good. And cotton comes from?"

"A plant?"

"Yes," said her mother. "These cotton plants only row in the hottest climates. The cotton plant stands the straightest in the hottest sun and, on one of the hottest days, the bud pops open, and out comes the cotton, kind of like popcorn."

"I like popcorn."

"I know. This reminds me of a story. When Bahá'u'lláh was older He had grandchildren . . ."

"Bahá'u'lláh was a grandfather?"

"Yes, and He enjoyed spending time with His grandchildren very much. They would often have picnics in a special garden called the Riḍván Garden, which His Son had purchased for Him. In that part of the world, in Israel, the sun is very hot, but Riḍván was lush and green with water and fountains.

"Was there cotton in the garden?"

"No, dear, but Bahá'u'lláh would send a servant to a city called Beirut to buy beautiful materials made from cotton and have dresses and other clothing sewn for His grandchildren."

"Mother, what do you think it would have been like to have Bahá'u'lláh as a grandfather?"

"Well, dear, I do know that Bahá'u'lláh's grandchildren loved their grandfather very much. He would always take an interest in whatever concerned them, and He knew lots of stories about Jesus Christ, Muḥammad, Moses, and other Prophets. The grandchildren would dress specially for Him because He loved perfection and order. Bahá'u'lláh had so much love in His heart, He could love anyone, even if the person hated Him."

"How could anyone hate Him, Mama? He seems like such a nice man, and He never did anyone any harm."

"Well, dear, some people had very difficult lives, and they knew nothing but envy and hate. Bahá'u'lláh was like a rose, and His love was like the fragrant perfume from the rose. The breeze carried this fragrance to everyone, whether it was to a friend or an enemy."

"That's nice, Mama. Roses are something else that like the summer heat, too, aren't they?"

"Yes, dear."

"Mama? I guess there are a lot of good things about summer, and I'll try not to complain when it gets too hot. I'll just try to find a cool place in the shade. Now, every time I smell a rose, I'll remember this night, and Bahá'u'lláh, and how we need to find that love in our hearts for everyone."

"And don't forget about yourself, dear. You are also very special, like the breeze that carries that fragrance."

"Thank you, Mama. I love you."

"I love you too, dear. Good night."

"Good night, Mama." ★

The Prison and the Garden

Written by Suzan Nadimi
Illustrated by Nina Scott

Bahá'u'lláh was born in a beautiful mansion lined with trees and flowering bushes. As a young boy, He spent His summers in a palace set among green mountains and valleys. But when He grew older, He was made a prisoner in a small dark cell with two narrow windows.

For two years, Bahá'u'lláh walked back and forth in His prison cell. Bahá'u'lláh then moved into a little white house, and for six more years, His only exercise was to pace the floor of His room.

He did not gaze at trees and flowering bushes. He did not look at green mountains and valleys. He paced back and forth, back and forth, over and over again.

When the prison doors opened, Bahá'u'lláh was free to live in a mansion with lovely trees and oranges like balls of fire.

In those free years, Bahá'u'lláh often asked to see His grandchildren before they went to bed. "Let the dear children come in, and have some dessert," He would say.

Some nights He would tell His grandchildren, "Now children, tomorrow you shall come with Me for a picnic to the Riḍván." On those nights the children's hearts were so filled with joy, they could hardly sleep.

Riḍván was a garden filled with flowering shrubs, sweet-smelling herbs, orange trees, and a splashing fountain. Together with His family and followers, Bahá'u'lláh would go to Riḍván and walk among pomegranate trees, white rosebushes, and bright red geraniums. He rested on a bench under the shade of a mulberry tree.

One day you might see the spot where Bahá'u'lláh sat on the bench under the mulberry tree. It is covered with beautiful potted plants. You might imagine Bahá'u'lláh sitting on the bench, surrounded by His grandchildren, saying, "Now children, tomorrow you shall come with Me for a picnic to the Riḍván." ★

He that bringeth up his son
or the son of another, it is as though
he hath brought up a son of Mine;
upon him rest My glory,
My loving-kindness, My mercy,
that have compassed the world.

— **Bahá'u'lláh,** *The Kitáb-i-Aqdas,* p. 37

The Power of Love

Written by Rick Johnson
Illustrated by Nina Scott

One Saturday, Charlie delivered pizza on a new street. He noticed a crowd of people standing in front of a well-tended house across the street. It was striking in contrast to the many run-down and abandoned houses around it. Curious, Charlie investigated.

Many children, youth, and adults were watching a performance. The wide front porch of the house was being used as a makeshift stage, and a large sign proclaimed:

Redma Street Bahá'í Community Center PRESENTS THE UNI-COMICAL PLAYERS — Music • Magic • Storytelling • Comedy — SUNDAY 10 AM

Charlie's attention was drawn to one of the actors in a very comical costume awaiting his turn to perform—Gomez, one of his classmates, in a red clown nose! What was he doing?

Gomez greeted him. "Hey there, Charlie—Great to see you!"

"Gomez! What's going on?" Charlie exclaimed.

"I'm a Bahá'í—that's my religion—and every Saturday we do this Uni-Comical Players thing here at the community center. You want to watch?"

"I'd like to stay, Gomez, but I'm working. I had no idea you lived around here."

"That's my mom," Gomez replied, "over there in the dog costume. Her name's Marian." He pointed to a performer in a large spotted dog costume on stage who was juggling several toasters!

"Marian's an amazing lady, Charlie," Gomez continued. "She and Pablo raised me after my parents died."

Charlie's head was spinning. "I've really gotta go, Gomez. I've got more deliveries."

Gomez smiled. "Come back when you get off. I'd really like you to meet my mom. We'll be tutoring here at the center 'til 6:00."

Charlie looked at the dog juggling on stage. "I'll be here by 3:30," Charlie grinned. As he completed his deliveries, he was full of new thoughts . . . and questions.

That afternoon, returning to the center, Charlie found Gomez sitting on the floor surrounded by children. He was telling a story.

"Hey, Charlie!" Gomez said. "Sit down, and I'll be done in a few minutes."

Charlie sat down and listened as Gomez continued, "So, the story about Áqá 'Abdu's-Ṣáliḥ, even though he lived a long way from here, inspires me because he had to deal with stuff similar to what I have to. He was an orphan, just like me. He had bullies bothering him, just like me in the school I go to. He had a really tough life and could have ended up beaten down and depressed like a lot of folks I know. But while he was still young, he decided to give his life to love rather than to anger. That turned him around. We can try to walk that path, too. Now, take your homework over to Marian—she's ready for you."

42   Bahá'u'lláh: Bahá'u'lláh and the Children of His Household

Gomez turned to Charlie. "Glad you made it, Charlie. I'm doing stories this afternoon. Mom says that the biggest problem with homework is getting the kids to believe it matters. These are smart kids, but sometimes they don't believe in themselves enough to do it. We use stories to help inspire them to do homework."

Charlie sighed. "Do you think it really works? Sometimes I wonder myself if homework matters. I'll probably be delivering pizzas the rest of my life! How is what you're doing going to change that? I've got nothing!"

"What if you have something wonderful inside, Charlie? Wouldn't that be something?" Gomez asked. "It's like with the story I just told—Áqá 'Abdu's-Ṣálih, as a youth, came to love Bahá'u'lláh—Whom Bahá'ís believe is a great Teacher sent by God—and Bahá'u'lláh's love convinced him he could overcome his problems. I learned the same thing when I lost my parents. It's like being trapped in a dark hole, and the only way out is that little tiny bit of sunlight that shows the way out. Bahá'u'lláh's love is that ray of light."

Bahá'u'lláh: Bahá'u'lláh and the Children of His Household

A gray-haired woman, about fifty, joined them. "Charlie, meet my mom, Mrs. Delgado—but folks call her Marian." Gomez smiled. "She keeps things moving here."

"Not so, Charlie," Marian laughed, "Love is the power that drives this place. Love can do many things that can't be done any other way."

"That's really the only reason I get anything done!" Gomez agreed. "Especially homework. As long as I can remember, we sat around as a family doing homework or reading, and that feeling of love and unity got me through. Some of these same stories were my favorites then."

"I guess that's why you do well in school?" Charlie asked curiously.

"Marian and Pablo gave me love, Charlie, and showed me that God is the source of that love. They inspired and encouraged me. They made me believe that I could do anything . . . so, that's pretty much what we try to do here at the center for the other kids."

"But it's hard, Gomez. I try, but sometimes I just feel overwhelmed. I struggle to help my Mom and sisters, but I'm not very strong . . ."

"Charlie," Marian spoke up, "it's more important how strong you can become than how strong you feel at the moment. How strong can you become, Charlie? That's the question."

Bahá'u'lláh: Bahá'u'lláh and the Children of His Household

"Come on, see how it works," Gomez invited.

Charlie went with Gomez as he began working with another group. "Everybody does a story station and ends with prayers, but they choose the homework or art stations they want."

Gomez told a story about Bahá'u'lláh's daughter, Bahíyyih Khánum. The story related how once, when she was a small girl and not very strong, she was asked to carry a heavy tea service upstairs for some visitors. "She performed this work with such a spirit of loving service that one of the visiting ladies said that the service of this small, weak girl was a proof of her religion. So, Bahíyyih's size and strength did not limit her ability to make a profound impact through her service. Even Bahá'u'lláh Himself wasn't big or strong," Gomez added. "Size wasn't a limit on Him at all—He has changed the hearts of millions of people in spite of His size."

"Even if we feel weak and limited," Gomez continued, "love can make us strong. When Bahá'u'lláh had a new granddaughter, some people wished she had been a boy, but Bahá'u'lláh said, 'I will love her more than the rest.' His love didn't look at what limitations people thought they had themselves or wanted to put on others. That's the power of love."

Later, as Charlie got ready to leave, he said, "Gomez, I'm not really sure what to think about all this, but I can see what you're doing. That gives me something to think about."

Charlie returned to the tutoring session the next day. Gomez waved at Charlie but kept talking to the children around him. "When we truly respect someone, we are never too busy for them and can always find time to show them we care. Sometimes, because they loved Him so, the children wanted to go to Bahá'u'lláh when other people thought He should not be disturbed. Bahá'u'lláh would welcome them anyway with love and sometimes give them sweets! He was never too busy for the little ones—'Let the dear children come in,' He would say."

Charlie began to see the process and began to try it himself. Gomez gradually helped him to begin telling stories to the children, and Marian taught him to juggle a little. Several weeks later, Charlie's mother and sisters came to the Uni-Comical Players' presentation on Saturday morning.

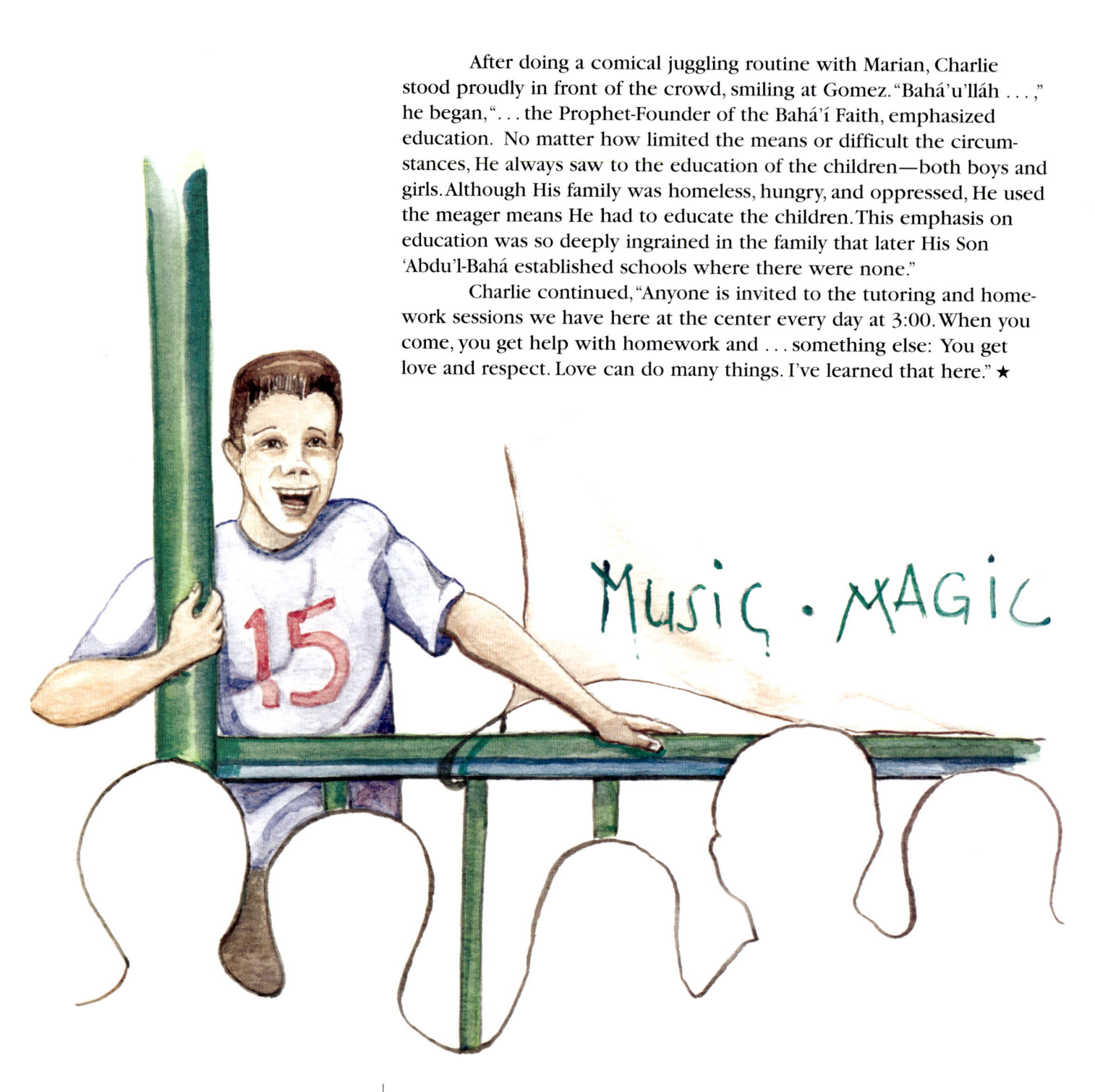

After doing a comical juggling routine with Marian, Charlie stood proudly in front of the crowd, smiling at Gomez. "Bahá'u'lláh . . . ," he began, ". . . the Prophet-Founder of the Bahá'í Faith, emphasized education. No matter how limited the means or difficult the circumstances, He always saw to the education of the children—both boys and girls. Although His family was homeless, hungry, and oppressed, He used the meager means He had to educate the children. This emphasis on education was so deeply ingrained in the family that later His Son 'Abdu'l-Bahá established schools where there were none."

Charlie continued, "Anyone is invited to the tutoring and homework sessions we have here at the center every day at 3:00. When you come, you get help with homework and . . . something else: You get love and respect. Love can do many things. I've learned that here." ★

Music · Magic

Bahá'u'lláh: Bahá'u'lláh and the Children of His Household

The Station of Bahá'u'lláh as Stated by 'Abdu'l-Bahá

4

> Verily, ye are the proofs of Bahá'u'lláh. Verily, Bahá'u'lláh is the True One, for He has trained such souls as these, each one of which is a proof in himself.
>
> — **'Abdu'l-Bahá**, *The Promulgation of Universal Peace*, p. 461

The Prisoner with Power

Written by Rick Johnson
Illustrated by Winifred Barnum-Newman

Julie felt it happening. Surprising things often happened during Bahá'í class that made her heart race fast. And it was happening again—ARRRGH! YAAAAAHHEE!—Julie's heart was racing a zillion beats a minute as she struggled with some heavy chain she was trying to break apart with her bare hands!

Each of the kids in the class had a piece of chain they were trying to break. Yells and grunts filled the air as they pulled at the chain with all their might. Gradually they got tired and fell to the floor, panting and giggling.

"So, kids, who was able to break one of the chains?" asked Ms. Bates, their teacher.

Bahá'u'lláh: The Station of Bahá'u'lláh as Stated by 'Abdu'l-Bahá | 49

The class laughed, because no one had been able to do it. "It's really hard," Willie said to the teacher. "I don't think anyone could do it, not even a grown up like you, Ms. Bates."

Ms. Bates picked up a piece of chain and struggled to break it, but had no success either. She held the chain up for everyone to see. "You're right, Willie, I can't do it either; none of us can. But Bahá'u'lláh did do something like breaking a chain—in fact, He did something even more amazing."

"'Abdu'l-Bahá says that one of the most important ways we can know that Bahá'u'lláh was a Prophet of God is that prisons and chains could not stop Him," Ms. Bates continued. "Although He was always a prisoner to the end of His life, He was not really in prison."

50 **Bahá'u'lláh:** The Station of Bahá'u'lláh as Stated by 'Abdu'l-Bahá

Now Julie's heart was really racing. It was like a riddle—How could you be a prisoner and yet not in prison? Julie thought, "What is Ms. Bates talking about?"

"Although not always in chains, Bahá'u'lláh was a prisoner for most of His adult life," Ms. Bates said. "In fact, the cruel king who sent Bahá'u'lláh to prison never wanted Bahá'u'lláh to go free. The king wanted Bahá'u'lláh to be kept in prison forever, always with a guard near Him and never having visitors. The king's plan was for Bahá'u'lláh to be so locked up that everyone would forget about Him. He thought that prison and chains could stop people from loving Bahá'u'lláh and wanting to learn from Him."

"But the king made a mistake, didn't he, Ms. Bates?" Stuart said, dropping his chain with a loud *clunk*.

"Yes, Stuart, the king was wrong," Ms. Bates said, smiling. "'Abdu'l-Bahá said that although the king never changed his mind about Bahá'u'lláh and always insisted that He remain a prisoner, after nine years in prison at 'Akká, Bahá'u'lláh walked out of the prison and took up residence in a mansion in the countryside."

"You mean He just walked out of prison and no one stopped Him?" Julie could not believe her ears!

"That's exactly right, Julie," Ms. Bates replied. "The jailers, officials, and people of 'Akká witnessed His leaving, but no one tried to stop Him. The people had come to love and respect Bahá'u'lláh so much that they wanted Him to be free. So, sometimes Bahá'u'lláh stayed at the Mansion of Bahjí, at other times He stayed at Mazra'ih, and other times He stayed in Haifa or pitched His tent on Mount Carmel."

"Bahá'u'lláh lived in a mansion? That's amazing! It's like He replaced the prison with a palace, didn't He?"

"That's right, Julie . . . What had been a life in chains became a walk in a beautiful garden. The attempt to silence Bahá'u'lláh and stop His teachings from spreading gave way to government officials and visitors coming to seek His advice. Nothing like this had ever happened before."

"Ms. Bates," Julie asked, "do you know what I think?"

"No, Julie, what?"

"That if Bahá'u'lláh can defeat a king while He's still a prisoner, He probably can do just about anything!"

"Yes, and we can ask Bahá'u'lláh to help us with our troubles, too, Julie," Ms. Bates added.

And that really made Julie's heart beat fast. ★

The Truth of Bahá'u'lláh's Mission

Written by Rick Johnson
Illustrated by Winifred Barnum-Newman

'Alí found a crown in Grandma's attic. It was dirty and bent, but it fit him perfectly!

"Gracious," Grandma laughed, "I wore that in a school play when I was ten!"

"Can I have it, please, Grandma?"

"Well," Grandma said, "don't you think that maybe your friends might like to have a crown like this, too?"

"But I want it myself," 'Alí cried.

"Well, 'Alí, let's clean it up and think about it."

Bahá'u'lláh: The Station of Bahá'u'lláh as Stated by 'Abdu'l-Bahá

When they finished cleaning up the crown, it dazzled! 'Alí was very happy. Then they made lots of his favorite cookies.

"Now, 'Alí," Grandma said, "let's invite your friends to meet us in the park. We'll eat cookies and let everyone wear the crown and parade around like kings and queens."

'Alí jumped around the room, whooping and hollering.

"You see, 'Alí," Grandma said, "what I want is for Bahá'u'lláh to be pleased with us. 'Abdu'l-Bahá said that there was no greater proof of the truth of Bahá'u'lláh's teachings than when we treat others with love and kindness. This is what Bahá'u'lláh wants us to do."

"Grandma," 'Alí said, "I'd probably be bored in a second if I had the crown all to myself."

Grandma hugged 'Alí close. "I know you didn't really want to keep the crown to yourself, 'Alí. Besides, don't you think that you all might attract some attention in the park?"

"The way we're going to march and sing," 'Alí laughed, "no one is going to miss the Kingdom of Bahá'u'lláh! " ★

Bahá'u'lláh: The Station of Bahá'u'lláh as Stated by 'Abdu'l-Bahá

> This is one of Bahá'u'lláh's greatest miracles: that He, a captive, surrounded Himself with panoply and He wielded power. The prison changed into a palace, the jail itself became a Garden of Eden. Such a thing has not occurred in history before . . .
>
> — 'Abdu'l-Bahá, *Memorials of the Faithful,* pp. 27–28

Bahá'u'lláh: The Station of Bahá'u'lláh as Stated by 'Abdu'l-Bahá

The Greatest Father-Son Story of All Time

Written by Rick Johnson
Illustrated by Winifred Barnum-Newman

When I was eleven, something wonderful happened. A new clerk appeared behind the counter at the corner store. It turned out that he and his wife had bought the grocery and were now living in the small apartment upstairs over the store. His name was Ken, and his wife's nickname was Bates.

I never saw a place change so fast! Almost any time of day, junk and dust were flying out the door—they were really cleaning the place up! A run-down convenience store became a place that had fresh cookies for kids after school.

Even my mom started coming by the grocery store to drink a soda with Bates on Sunday mornings. It wasn't long until she and Bates were friends, and they'd spend hours talking together.

Bahá'u'lláh: The Station of Bahá'u'lláh as Stated by 'Abdu'l-Bahá

I was so lucky! On Sunday mornings, while Mom and Bates talked, I'd watch Ken play chess with some of the senior citizens. And when Ken had to serve a customer, he'd say to me, "OK, Chip, you take over for a couple of turns!" I felt so proud to be sitting across the chessboard from old Mr. Scroggins. I usually held my own, although I did lose Ken's queen a couple of times. But he didn't seem to mind, and sometimes it seemed that Ken let me play most of a game, kind of like he was making work for himself to let me go on. I liked that.

About the third month that Mom and I spent Sunday mornings at the store, I asked Ken what made him so special. I just couldn't get out of my head what a difference he and Bates had made in such a short time.

"Well," Ken responded, "if it's OK with your mom, I'll introduce you to someone who helps me—His name is 'Abdu'l-Bahá."

I asked my Mom if I could meet this special friend of Ken's, and she smiled at Bates and gave her one of those "I-know-what-you're-thinking" looks, and said, "Maybe I could 'meet' Him too, since we were just talking about the same thing."

Ken took us behind the counter, and there, hanging on the wall in their tiny office, was a picture of a man with a long white beard and a kind of funny turban-style hat. It looked a little strange for our neighborhood, but He had the happiest eyes I'd ever seen—except maybe for Ken and Bates. So this was where the sparkle in their eyes came from!

"This is 'Abdu'l-Bahá," Ken told me. He leaned over to me and whispered, "He's my coach when I need to know how to beat you at chess." The twinkle in his eyes told me he was teasing me.

Bahá'u'lláh: The Station of Bahá'u'lláh as Stated by 'Abdu'l-Bahá

"Come on, Ken, tell me who He is *really*," I pleaded.

Ken said that 'Abdu'l-Bahá taught that there was love in everybody's heart just waiting to get out if we let it. He said that the more people let the love out of their hearts, the better the world would be.

"But, Ken, you and Bates are only two people."

Ken said that even a few people doing it would make the town better and happier. So, they thought they'd work on this one little corner in our neighborhood. "And, Chip, you and your mom are regulars here now, so there are at least four of us now— that's a 100 percent improvement already!"

Well, he had me there. I told him that I guessed it could work.

"But the neat thing, Chip, is that we both have more love we can let out of our hearts, and 'Abdu'l-Bahá shows us how to do it.

"Come on, Chip, I'll show you what I mean. We're going to plant some flowers out in front of the store. You can help."

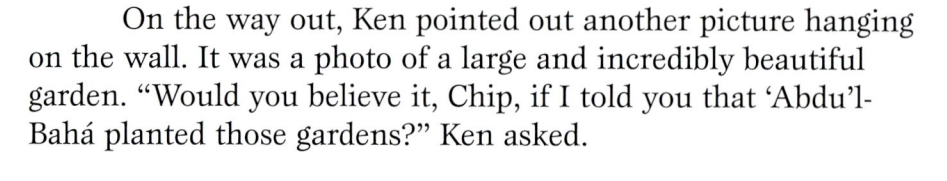

On the way out, Ken pointed out another picture hanging on the wall. It was a photo of a large and incredibly beautiful garden. "Would you believe it, Chip, if I told you that 'Abdu'l-Bahá planted those gardens?" Ken asked.

"Oh, Ken, you're teasing me again!" I laughed.

"No, I'm not teasing you, Chip," Ken replied. "Those gardens are around the grave of 'Abdu'l-Bahá's Father, Whose name was Bahá'u'lláh. 'Abdu'l-Bahá loved Bahá'u'lláh so much that He started planting those gardens over 100 years ago, and that is what they look like today. When He began, it was almost like a desert! It took lots of people and many years for it to become so beautiful, but 'Abdu'l-Bahá began it all."

As we continued outside, I saw that Ken was bringing along some big buckets. "OK, Chip, there's hardly any dirt out here, and there's no water, so we'll have to haul some dirt from the alley in back of the store and then carry water from the back storeroom. That's what the buckets are for."

It was really amazing that Ken saw something useful in the weedy alley behind the store. What a mess it was!

We carried soil, bucket by bucket, to the front of the store and poured it into some flower boxes Bates had prepared. Then we carried water from the storeroom.

Getting dirt and water in my socks was so much fun! It was better than finding a dollar bill on the sidewalk, even if the buckets were heavy!

"This is our little gardening project inspired by 'Abdu'l-Bahá," Bates said. She told about how much 'Abdu'l-Bahá loved Bahá'u'lláh, and said that one of the ways 'Abdu'l-Bahá showed this love was to create gardens around the Shrine of Bahá'u'lláh.

"People often saw 'Abdu'l-Bahá carrying heavy pots of water, with sweat pouring off His face, as He planted those gardens," Bates said as she patted the dirt around the flowers. "He even carried soil in His cloak to where He was working. 'Abdu'l-Bahá wanted to show His love for Bahá'u'lláh so much that He did not seem to notice the hard work—even though He was over seventy years old."

"Here comes some more water!" I yelled, running with the bucket, water sloshing merrily into my shoes.

"How in the world did 'Abdu'l-Bahá do it?" Mom asked.

"Sometimes He walked two miles carrying flower pots on His shoulders," Ken said. "Can you imagine Him, white hair and beard flowing, carrying these flower pots down the dusty roads of old Palestine?"

"I'll bet the neighbors thought He was crazy," I blurted out.

"I'd say, not crazy, but in love with Bahá'u'lláh," Bates said. "I think it was the greatest Father-Son story of all time.

Bahá'u'lláh: The Station of Bahá'u'lláh as Stated by 'Abdu'l-Bahá | 61

"One time, 'Abdu'l-Bahá's legs got so stiff from standing and working the water pump handle that He couldn't walk, and his friends had to carry Him away from the pump and rub His legs. "Abdu'l-Bahá,' they asked Him, 'why do you tire yourself so?' Do you know what He answered? 'What can I do for Bahá'u'lláh?' There just seemed to be no difficulty that could limit His service to Bahá'u'lláh. The more He remembered Bahá'u'lláh, the more He wanted to serve."

"You were telling me that the gardens 'Abdu'l-Bahá started are now one of the wonders of the world," my Mom said.

"Yes," Ken said, "He turned a desert into a garden."

"Well, this corner wasn't a desert exactly, but I'd say it was close enough," I laughed. "I guess I see your point about how 'Abdu'l-Bahá's gardening inspired what you are doing here on this corner."

"We just think that we're letting a little love out of our hearts in what we're doing here, and you are too," Bates said. "Little by little, that love will show up in the flowers; and little by little, people will notice."

"And pretty soon they'll be helping with the gardening!"

"Yes, Chip," Ken laughed, "there's a lot of room for more flower gardens on this block!" ★

Bahá'u'lláh: The Station of Bahá'u'lláh as Stated by 'Abdu'l-Bahá

The Childhood of Bahá'u'lláh

5

> "He Who is the Best-Beloved is come!"
>
> — **Bahá'u'lláh**,
> *Gleanings from the Writings of Bahá'u'lláh*, p. 319

Bahá'u'lláh: The Childhood of Bahá'u'lláh

Bahá'u'lláh's Fishes

Written by Rick Johnson
Illustrated by Cindy Pacileo

My big sister Maggie is excited and chatters constantly. She's leaving for Africa today to do a Bahá'í year of service.

I'm not excited. I'll miss Maggie. She's my best friend, although she's twelve years older. Doug and Mollie, who are in between, are great, but somehow Maggie and I have always been best buddies. She and I raise calves, pigs, sheep, and goats together. We're a team and always win ribbons at the fair. *

---

* On farms in the United States, young children may help with the farm work. Even toddlers begin to help care for animals, and younger children assist older siblings showing animals in county fair competitions.

Bahá'u'lláh: The Childhood of Bahá'u'lláh

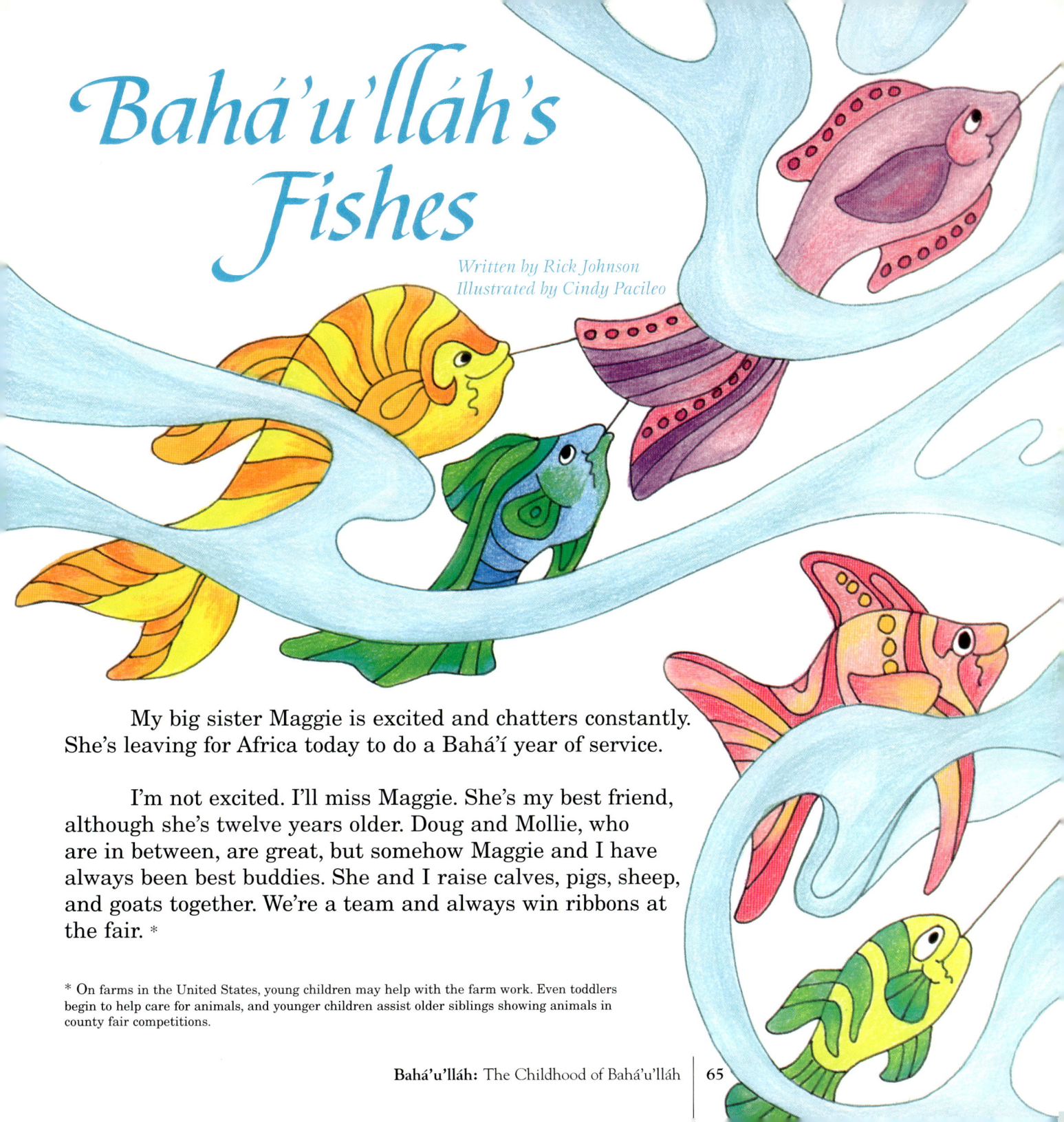

Now she's going off to serve in an agricultural development project. She wants to learn how they farm in Africa and share what she knows about farming. After her year of service, she's going to college, and then she'll be the first of us kids to begin taking over the farm from Papa. I understand that, but I'll still miss her.

"Maggie," I tell her, clinging to her neck, "I'll worry about you every day. I'd be scared if I were you!"

Maggie hugs me. "Ellie," she says, stroking my hair, "I'll be fine. Tonight, you ask Mama to tell you the 'fishes story,' and when she does, you think about me. That'll prove to you I'll be fine."

That night, when I go to bed, I feel a little sad. "Mama," I say, "will you tell me the fishes story? Maggie promised it would make me not worry about her."

"All right, Ellie," Mama says. "You snuggle down. Then, after the story, right to sleep."

"Now, you know," she began, "that when Bahá'u'lláh was five or six, He had dreams in which birds of the air and fishes of the sea were attacking Him from all sides, but none of them could hurt Him. A famous interpreter of dreams explained that the dreams meant that Bahá'u'lláh would found a great cause and, despite attacks from enemies, would always be victorious."

"But Mama, that's not the fishes story!"

"Yes, Ellie, I know," Mama replies, "but I wanted you to see that there were several stories about similar dreams that tell us the same thing about Bahá'u'lláh—that He had the unfailing protection of God. With help from God, no problem was too big for Bahá'u'lláh to overcome. So, when I tell you the fishes story, you remember that there are several stories like it. That assures us even more that Bahá'u'lláh is stronger than loneliness, or fear, or troubles."

"So, Bahá'u'lláh will keep Maggie safe, too, Mama?"

"That's where the fishes come in, Ellie. Mírzá Buzurg, the father of Bahá'u'lláh, dreamed that Bahá'u'lláh was swimming in a vast ocean, bigger than any other ocean anywhere. As He swam, His long, jet-black hair floated out in all directions. Great schools of fish swam around Him on all sides, each one holding onto the end of one hair. Can you imagine such a thing, Ellie?"

Bahá'u'lláh: The Childhood of Bahá'u'lláh

"No, Mama," I say, covering my eyes, "that would be really scary!" It's a little game we play. I pretend to be scared during this part of the story, and then giggle like crazy when the good part comes!

"Well, you don't have to be scared for Bahá'u'lláh, Ellie, because the story's not over yet," Mama smiles at me with my eyes peeking out between my fingers.

"So, in the dream there were thousands of fishes hanging on Bahá'u'lláh's hair. But no matter how many fish there were, or how hard they pulled on His hair, Bahá'u'lláh just kept swimming as if nothing were happening! They could not hurt one single hair on His head! He just swam along peacefully as if He were completely free."

"So Maggie can do that, too, can't she Mama? She can be like Bahá'u'lláh!"

"Well, honey, she can't really be like Bahá'u'lláh," Mama replied, "but when she calls on Bahá'u'lláh for help, He uses that same power He had over those fishes in the dream."

"And Bahá'u'lláh's father stopped worrying about Him, didn't he, Mama?"

"Yes, a person who knew about dreams told him that it meant that the fishes represented all the peoples of the earth gathering around Bahá'u'lláh and clinging to Him. His calm and powerful swimming among them is a symbol of the power and protection of God that helps Him."

"And we're like all the little fishes clinging to Him!" This is the part of the story I really like, and I start making fish faces and waving my arms like fins.

"Maggie will be just fine, Ellie, because she's Bahá'u'lláh's fish. No matter where she is, as long as she holds onto Him, she'll be okay."

"Mama, I want to be like Maggie. I want to go to Africa and Asia and New Mexico and everywhere!"

Mama laughs and holds me close. "Angel, you will be Bahá'u'lláh's best fish!"

"I'll be a whale, Mama! That's how much I love Bahá'u'lláh!" ★

Bahá'u'lláh Is Born

Written by Suzan Nadimi
Illustrated by Cindy Pacileo

In the early hours of dawn of the twelfth day of November 1817, in the city of Ṭihrán, in the land of Persia, a baby boy named Mírzá Ḥusayn-'Alí was born to a loving father and mother.

Bahá'u'lláh: The Childhood of Bahá'u'lláh

He had two eyes, like His father.
He had two lips, like His mother.
He had two hands, like His sister.
He had two legs, like His brother.
But in His heart He had a Spirit, a most glorious, wondrous Spirit, unlike any other.

So when that baby boy grew to be a man, and His name became Bahá'u'lláh,
    eyes cried softly in His presence,
    lips sang sweetly His praise,
    hands held gently His Tablets,
    legs walked tirelessly to see Him, and
    hearts glowed brightly in His love.

However, in the early hours of dawn of the twelfth day of November 1817, in the city of Ṭihrán, in the land of Persia, He was a baby boy just born to a loving father and mother: a baby with two eyes, two lips, two hands and two legs—and they loved Him. ★

*The everlasting Candle
shineth in its naked glory.
Behold how it hath
consumed every mortal veil.
O ye moth-like lovers of His light!
Brave every danger,
and consecrate your souls
to its consuming flame.*

— **Bahá'u'lláh,** *Gleanings from the Writings of Bahá'u'lláh,* p. 321

Illustrated by Cindy Pacileo, design inspired by Barbara Trauger-Querry

Bahá'u'lláh: The Childhood of Bahá'u'lláh

The Puppet Show

Written by Suzan Nadimi
Illustrated by Cindy Pacileo

Jacob walked into the kitchen with his hair combed, face washed, and his book *Stories of Bahá'u'lláh* in hand. There he found his father, sitting behind the table, gazing through the window and drinking coffee.

"DAD! You're not ready!" said Jacob.

"The building contractor just called to say he was coming over," Jacob's father replied. "I'm afraid you'll have to miss class."

Jacob reminded his father of his promise to take him to Bahá'í class this week. That's why 'Alí's parents hadn't come to pick him up.

"I know your mother and I haven't taken you to class lately," Jacob's father said. "We've been so busy working overtime and planning for the renovation. But imagine spending time together in our bigger home, sitting by the fire, playing games, and reading books. Just think about it!"

Jacob didn't want to think about it. He wanted to go to class. He thought of Peter, Ryan, and 'Alí playing dodge ball without him. He saw them munching on the freshly baked cookies their teacher, Ms. Gomez, always brought. He imagined them play-acting the puppet show Bahá'u'lláh had seen as a young boy about a king and his princes, servants, and soldiers.

"And I was going to be the king," Jacob muttered to himself.

As courteously and emphatically as he could, Jacob expressed his desire to attend Bahá'í class. Gently and firmly, Jacob's father informed him that the contractor was not to be missed.

"The contractor's a very busy man," he said. "We're lucky he's agreed to see us today."

"We can still make it to class if the meeting doesn't last too long," Jacob said. "I'll just miss the cookies and the prayers."

Jacob's father replied that he expected the meeting to last a long time.

Jacob ran to dial 'Alí's number. Nobody picked up the phone. "They must've left already," Jacob said to himself.

"Please help me get to class, Bahá'u'lláh," Jacob prayed. Then he sat down at the table to think.

74 **Bahá'u'lláh:** The Childhood of Bahá'u'lláh

Before long, Jacob's thoughts wandered to the story in his book about the puppet show. In the show, puppets dressed as servants rushed out of a tent calling, "The King is coming! The King is coming!" The puppet-king, in his royal robe and dazzling crown, strutted upon the scene, followed by his ministers and soldiers. Trumpets blared. Shots were fired into the air. Smoke filled the tent. The puppet-king showed off his glory and power by ordering soldiers, ministers, and princes this way and that. After the show was over, a man emerged from behind the tent carrying a box under his arm.

Jacob opened his book and read where Bahá'u'lláh asked the man, "What is this box?"

The man replied, "All these lavish trappings, the king, the princes, and the ministers, their pomp and glory, their might and power—everything that you saw—are all now contained within this box."

The moral of the story was, Ms. Gomez had told his class, that nothing belonging to this world is important because one day everything will end up in a box.

"I wish Bahá'u'lláh could come tell my dad that our bigger house isn't more important than going to Bahá'í class," Jacob thought.

Suddenly he had an idea! He pushed his book toward his father and asked, "Could you please read this story, Dad? I need to practice my part. I'm going to be the king."

Jacob's father read the story, at first glancing at the kitchen door every so often, but soon forgetting to do so.

Bahá'u'lláh: The Childhood of Bahá'u'lláh

He read out loud, "'Erelong these outward trappings, these heaped-up treasures, these earthly vanities . . . this gorgeous finery . . . all shall pass into the confines of the grave, as though into that box.'"

"Bahá'u'lláh was a very wise boy to see that none of those things mattered," said Jacob's father when he finished the story. "Okay! Let's go to Bahá'í class!"

Just then the contractor approached the kitchen door.

"But what about your meeting?" Jacob asked.

"I'm going to ask the contractor if we could start the meeting in the car so I can drop you off," Jacob's father said. "After all, our bigger house isn't more important than going to Bahá'í class, is it?" ★

The Youth and Early Manhood of Bahá'u'lláh

6

> Look upon this Youth, O King, with the eyes of justice; judge thou, then, with truth concerning what hath befallen Him.

— Bahá'u'lláh, *The Proclamation of Bahá'u'lláh*, p. 58

The Bada<u>sh</u>t Conference

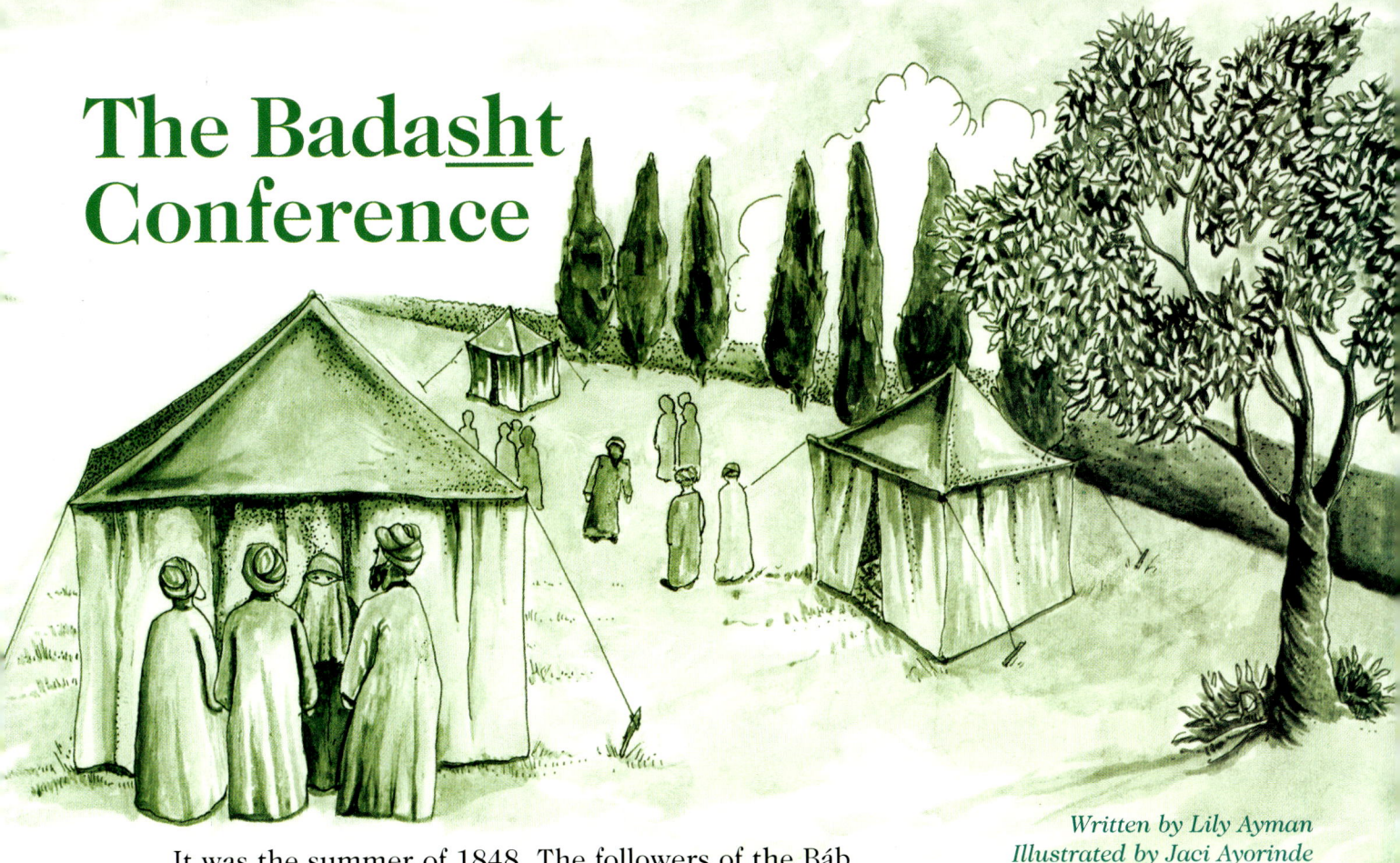

Written by Lily Ayman
Illustrated by Jaci Ayorinde

It was the summer of 1848. The followers of the Báb, the Bábís, were fiercely persecuted in Persia, the birthplace of their Faith. They needed guidance and support. Bahá'u'lláh, Who, at that time, was a directing force among the Bábís, decided to meet with His fellow believers. A group of them gathered in the small village of Bada<u>sh</u>t in northern Persia.

Upon His arrival, Bahá'u'lláh rented three gardens, one for Quddús, another for Qurratu'l-'Ayn, and the third one for Himself. The main purpose of this gathering of Bábís, known as the Bada<u>sh</u>t Conference, was to consult about the future of the Bábí Faith. Tents were put up in the three gardens to house the eighty-one Bábís who had gathered at this most important event. From the day they arrived to the day they left, for twenty-two days, they were all the guests of Bahá'u'lláh.

Bahá'u'lláh: The Youth and Early Manhood of Bahá'u'lláh | 79

Every day, Bahá'u'lláh revealed a new Tablet, which was chanted every morning in this memorable gathering of Bábís. Through these Tablets, Bahá'u'lláh discarded one after another of the established traditions of the past. The Bábís were dismayed as they saw the ways they had worshiped, and many of the teachings they had followed for so long, changed and discarded.

Bahá'u'lláh bestowed a new name on every believer at Badasht without disclosing the identity of the person who had given those names. From this time on, He became known as "Bahá" (Glory), Quddús (the Most Holy) gained his title, and Qurrat'u-'Ayn became known as "Ṭáhirih" (the Pure).

The Bábís were in awe. They did not know the source of all these Revelations. They wondered: Who wrote the Tablets? Who gave them the new names? Some were guessing, each one to his own degree of understanding. Very few, if any, thought Bahá'u'lláh was the author of the changes that were so fearlessly introduced.

Bahá'u'lláh presided every day over the Conference of Badasht, guiding the discussions and enlightening His fellow believers. Ṭáhirih and Quddús, encouraged by Bahá'u'lláh, discussed the future of the Bábí Revelation. Ṭáhirih wanted to declare its complete break from Islam. Quddús rejected her views. Bahá'u'lláh did not take sides but let the two examine and contemplate all aspects of this most important matter.

One day, Bahá'u'lláh was not feeling well and decided to remain in His garden. As soon as Quddús heard this news, he went to His presence. Gradually other believers came too and gathered around Him. Suddenly, a messenger from Ṭáhirih came and addressed Quddús saying, "Ṭáhirih wants to meet with you in her garden."

"I do not wish to meet with her anymore!" exclaimed Quddús bluntly.

The messenger refused to return without him. Suddenly, Ṭáhirih appeared at the door. Beautifully adorned, she stood serenely before her companions. She was not wearing her veil, a requirement for women under the laws of Islam.

Immediately, the men stood up in complete shock, as if struck by lightning. An honorable woman appearing without a veil! How could they gaze on the unveiled face of the one whom they considered the best example of purity, honor, and modesty? One of them cut his throat and fled the place with some others following him. Some not only left the conference, but they also left the Faith they had been ready to defend. Such was their degree of attachment to the traditions of the past and their anger toward Ṭáhirih's brave action!

Those who remained listened in complete awe to Ṭáhirih's eloquent speech delivered in a language highly resembling that of the Qur'án, the Holy Book of Islam. In her address, she announced the dawn of a New Day. She announced that this was the time to break away from the traditions of the past. She ended her talk in her strong, melodious voice, declaring: "This is the day in which the fetters of the past are burst asunder."

This incident changed the life of the Bábís. The change involved all their manners and customs. It freed them from the obligation of following the Muslim clergy. Yet they remained confused. Many of them wrote letters to the Báb, asking for guidance. Each one of them received a Tablet from Him reassuring them and confirming the changes. In regard to Ṭáhirih's unveiled appearance, He wrote, "What am I to say regarding her whom the Tongue of Power and Glory [Bahá'u'lláh] has named Ṭáhirih [the Pure One]." By writing this, He also showed that Ṭáhirih's appearance, unveiled in the presence of men, was acceptable.

Bahá'u'lláh, with His love, wisdom, and patience, built peace and harmony among the remaining believers at Badasht. The main objective of the gathering was achieved; the future of the Bábí Faith was determined. "The clarion-call of the new Order had been sounded. . . . The way was clear for the proclamation of the laws and precepts that were destined to usher in the new Dispensation."* ★

---

* Nabíl, *The Dawn-Breakers*, pp. 297–98

Lives of Service

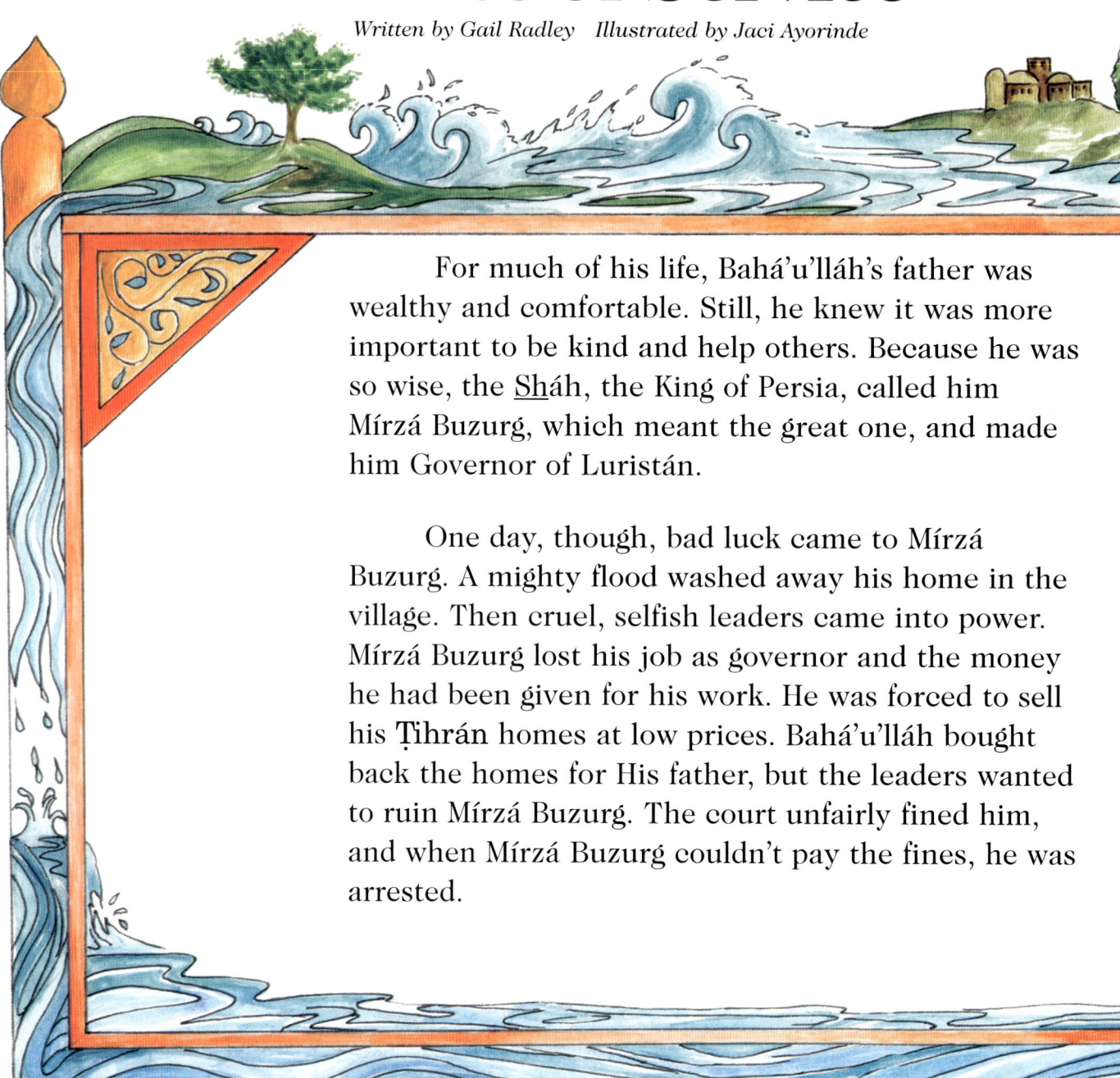

Written by Gail Radley   Illustrated by Jaci Ayorinde

For much of his life, Bahá'u'lláh's father was wealthy and comfortable. Still, he knew it was more important to be kind and help others. Because he was so wise, the S͟háh, the King of Persia, called him Mírzá Buzurg, which meant the great one, and made him Governor of Luristán.

One day, though, bad luck came to Mírzá Buzurg. A mighty flood washed away his home in the village. Then cruel, selfish leaders came into power. Mírzá Buzurg lost his job as governor and the money he had been given for his work. He was forced to sell his Ṭihrán homes at low prices. Bahá'u'lláh bought back the homes for His father, but the leaders wanted to ruin Mírzá Buzurg. The court unfairly fined him, and when Mírzá Buzurg couldn't pay the fines, he was arrested.

Bahá'u'lláh: The Youth and Early Manhood of Bahá'u'lláh

Bahá'u'lláh knew He had to help His father. He rode to Ṭihrán to insist that the fines be dropped and the dishonest collector dismissed. Then Bahá'u'lláh rented a home so that He could take care of His family and many needy relatives. Although Bahá'u'lláh's father was no longer wealthy and powerful, he continued to help others however he could for the rest of his life.

When Mírzá Buzurg died, friends hoped Bahá'u'lláh would become governor, knowing He would be wise and fair as His father had been. To their surprise, Bahá'u'lláh refused.

"Leave Him to Himself," the prime minister said. "Such a position is unworthy of Him."

None of them knew then that Mírzá Buzurg's son would help all people as the Promised One. ★

The effulgence of the Abhá Beauty hath pierced the veil of night; behold the souls of His lovers dancing, moth-like, in the light that has flashed from His face.

— Ṭáhirih, in *The Dawn-Breakers*, p. 286

Escape to Ṭihrán

Written by Jean Gould
Illustrated by Jaci Ayorinde

    Bahá'u'lláh knew that Ṭáhirih was in trouble. Probably any intelligent, outspoken woman in Persia at the beginning of Ramaḍán, the Muslim period of fasting, in 1847, would be in trouble. Women in Persia in 1847 were expected to remain silent and behind their veils. A beautiful, courageous poetess who had proven herself so capable of convincing people to join her in following the Báb would be in serious trouble, however.

    It began in Qazvín when Mullá Taqí, Ṭáhirih's uncle and father-in-law, tried to force her to give up her faith in the Báb and return to her husband, who shared his father's malice for the Báb and His followers. The husband expected her to always obey him, to keep quiet, and limit her attentions to traditional womanly concerns. When she refused to meet these demands, her uncle became so angry that he struck the beautiful Ṭáhirih—not once, but several times. Into the silence that followed this terrible moment, she suddenly cried, "O Uncle, I see your mouth fill up with blood." These prophetic words heralded a catastrophic chain of events.

It wasn't long before Mullá Taqí, who had certainly disregarded the words of a mere woman, was in the mosque one morning at dawn where he was soon to lead the people in prayer. As he knelt on his prayer rug, a man suddenly rushed from the shadows, threw the Mullá onto his back, and plunged a dagger into his mouth. Then he ran away into the dark while Mullá Taqí lay in a growing pool of blood that flowed from between his lips.

The killer was a follower of Shaykh Aḥmad and Siyyid Kázim, holy men who had foretold the coming of the Báb. He had been on his way to try to secure an audience with the Báb when he came across a ruthless mob tormenting a fellow Shaykhí. When he learned that Mullá Taqí had issued the order for the torment, he formed his simple, deadly plan and carried it through immediately.

When the real killer could not be found, Ṭáhirih's enraged husband and his relatives were delighted to accuse Ṭáhirih, the Pure One, of orchestrating the death of her father-in-law. "No one else but you is guilty of the murder of our father," they accused. "You issued the order for his assassination."

They managed to imprison Ṭáhirih in her father's house and surround her with women who were instructed to keep her in her room, except to perform her ablutions, when she washed for prayers. This was certainly not enough for a pack of relatives thirsting for blood. They demanded that many Bábís must die to pay for the death of Mullá Taqí.

The Muslim leaders and their followers joined the relatives in the hunt. Together, they sprang upon defenseless victims and used appallingly creative ways to slaughter them—men, women, and children—with no mercy and certainly no fear of reprisal.

Some Bábís were put into chains, herded to Ṭihrán, and imprisoned in the house of one of the headmen, or kad-khudá, as they were called. It was then that Bahá'u'lláh entered this particular fray. Ever the Father of the Poor, ever the Champion of the oppressed, He determined to intervene on behalf of His fellow Bábís.

"Oh, yes," said the greedy kad-khudá when Bahá'u'lláh came to see him. "They are destitute of the barest necessities of life. They hunger for food, and their clothing is wretchedly scanty." When, at Bahá'u'lláh's command, the money and food began to pour into the house, the kad-khudá informed his superiors, who saw the perfect opportunity to take advantage of Bahá'u'lláh's legendary generosity.

They summoned Bahá'u'lláh to their presence. They protested His actions and accused Him of partnership in the murder of Mullá Taqí. "The kad-khudá," Bahá'u'lláh replied, "pleaded their cause before Me and enlarged upon their sufferings and needs. He himself bore witness to their innocence and appealed to Me for help. In return for the aid, which in response to his invitation, I was impelled to extend, you now charge Me with a crime of which I am innocent."

They ignored Bahá'u'lláh's logic. It wasn't their purpose to learn the truth, and they refused to allow Him to return home. They demanded the outrageous sum of one thousand túmáns for His release.

Within a few days, these friends intervened on His behalf and used powerful words to threaten the kad-khudá and his greedy cohorts. Soon they were forced to hand over Bahá'u'lláh, along with a thousand apologies. The one thousand túmáns were never mentioned again.

Bahá'u'lláh's work was only beginning. In Qazvín, Ṭáhirih was living under terrible conditions. She was refusing food because her husband and his relatives had poisoned it, and she fretted in her "cage," grieving for the loss of so many friends. Now, her husband had determined that she should somehow suffer the same bloody fate, and he began to plot in earnest.

But Ṭáhirih, the Pure, the Fearless, had had enough. She had a steadfast and unmovable faith in a higher and unconquerable Power. With her formidable mind, she had recognized the station of Bahá'u'lláh and His ability to achieve the seemingly impossible. In her darkest hour, she issued a challenge to her husband: "If my Cause be the Cause of Truth, if the Lord I worship be none other than the one true God, He will, ere nine days have elapsed, deliver me from the yoke of your tyranny. Should He fail to achieve my deliverance, you are free to act as you desire. You will have irrevocably established the falsity of my belief."

The cowardly husband, unable to accept so bold a challenge, ignored it completely and continued his scheming ways.

Bahá'u'lláh heard and accepted the challenge, however, and determined to establish the truth of her words. From His home in the capital city of Ṭihrán, He orchestrated her escape with a wonderfully simple plan. Muḥammad-Hádí, the faithful, eldest brother of Ṭáhirih, was summoned to Bahá'u'lláh's presence and entrusted with the plan. "The Almighty will assuredly guide your steps and will surround you with His unfailing protection," He said.

Muḥammad-Hádí set out immediately for Qazvín. There

he enlisted the help of his wife, K͟hátúm-Ján, who was devoted to Ṭáhirih and who had become a genius at finding ways to contact her and bring her food. This time, according to divine plan, she dressed in disguise as a beggar woman to deliver a heavenly letter. After reading its fateful contents, Ṭáhirih whispered, "You go, and I will follow." In a little while, the Pure One joined her. Miraculously, they passed from the house unnoticed. Veiled and unhindered by people or possessions, they stepped quietly through the streets past an unsuspecting populace to the house of a carpenter, a friend of Muḥammad-Hádí's and K͟hátúm-Ján's, where no lady of high status would deign to go.

Within the hour, the alarm was raised. Ṭáhirih the Bold had indeed disappeared. When the news spread, the people and the Muslim clergy raised a great cry. Under cover of night and confusion, the three friends fled to the S͟háhzádih Gate and flew on wings of fear and joy past the city walls to the abattoir, the slaughterhouse, where there waited three horses to carry them away to Ṭihrán, the city of light. Leaping onto the backs of the willing animals, the trio rode away into the darkness. Later, exhausted but triumphant, they reached the outskirts of the capital as the day began to break. There they stopped in an empty garden to rest and hide.

When night fell, several horsemen stealthily entered the garden to pay their respects to the Pure One and deliver a final instruction. Once more, Ṭáhirih mounted her horse, and together they rode to the city gates, where they slipped through unnoticed and unrecognized. Soon Baha'u'lláh's vast and glittering house came into view. A door quietly opened, and Ṭáhirih the Beautiful slipped from her horse, stepped across the threshold, and passed beyond the bounds of prying eyes. For the moment, she was safe within the strong fortress created by Bahá'u'lláh, the Father of the Poor, and His wife, the Mother of Consolation. ★

Bahá'u'lláh: The Youth and Early Manhood of Bahá'u'lláh

Principles Related to the Oneness of God and the Oneness of Humanity

7

The tabernacle of unity
hath been raised;
regard ye not one another as strangers.
Ye are the fruits of one tree,
and the leaves of one branch.

— **Bahá'u'lláh**, Gleanings from the Writings of Bahá'u'lláh, p. 218

Illustrated by Carrie Kneisler

Isfandíyár

Written by Patricia R. Tomarelli
Illustrated by Keith Kresge

In 1912, 'Abdu'l-Bahá gave a talk in Washington, D.C. In those days in North America, it was unusual for people of African descent and people of European descent to gather together in the same meeting. 'Abdu'l-Bahá said that He was very happy that day, because Bahá'u'lláh teaches that we are all one human family. He declared, "In the sight of God there is no distinction between whites and blacks; all are as one. Anyone whose heart is pure is dear to God—whether white or black, red or yellow."

Bahá'u'lláh: Principles Related to the Oneness of God and the Oneness of Humanity

Then He told a story about Isfandíyár, a man who served Bahá'u'lláh with perfect faithfulness. After telling the story, 'Abdu'l-Bahá explained, "Then, it is evident that excellence does not depend upon color. Character is the true criterion of humanity."

Here is a retelling of the story that 'Abdu'l-Bahá told that day:

There once was a man—a perfect man—
who served Bahá'u'lláh and
whom I loved very much,
and his name was Isfandíyár.

When Bahá'u'lláh was in prison,
the King of Persia wanted to know
His secrets, so he sent more than
one hundred policemen to find Isfandíyár.

"Isfandíyár, Isfandíyár,
where do you go, Isfandíyár?"

96 | **Bahá'u'lláh:** Principles Related to the Oneness of God and the Oneness of Humanity

"I go to the market to sell my things."

"Isfandíyár, Isfandíyár,
why do you go, Isfandíyár?"

"I sell my things to pay my debts."

"But Isfandíyár, Isfandíyár,
those are not your debts.
They are the debts of Bahá'u'lláh."

"Ah yes! And if I do not pay,
the people will say that
a servant of Bahá'u'lláh
has bought and used
the goods and supplies
of the storekeepers
and did not pay for them."

Bahá'u'lláh: Principles Related to the Oneness of God and the Oneness of Humanity

"Oh Isfandíyár, Isfandíyár, for you I am afraid."

"I am not."

"There are over one hundred policemen looking for you."

"I must do this."

"If they catch you, with fire they will torture you."

"I must do this."

"They will cut off your fingers."

"I must do this."

"They will cut off your ears."

"I must do this".

"They will put out your eyes so you will tell the secrets of Bahá'u'lláh."

"I must do this."

"Go away."

"No."

"Do not remain."

"No."

"Oh, Isfandíyár,
I am so afraid."

"I am not.
If they take me, never mind.

"If they punish me,
there is no harm.

"I must remain until I pay
all that is owed.
Then I will go."

"Oh, Isfandíyár, Isfandíyár,
where are you now?"

"I am with my Beloved."

"Isfandíyár, Isfandíyár,
how are you now, Isfandíyár?"

"I am a point of light.
I am the essence of love.
I am the faithful servant of Bahá'u'lláh." ★

Retold from a talk by 'Abdu'l-Bahá in *The Promulgation of Universal Peace,* pp. 425–26

Bahá'u'lláh: Principles Related to the Oneness of God and the Oneness of Humanity | 99

A Journey Across a Desert

Written by Gail Radley
Illustrated by Carrie Kneisler

If you crossed a hot, dry desert with little to drink, think how happy a cool fountain at the end would make you. This is how happy 'Abdu'l-Bahá says Bahá'ís should feel when they meet each other. Bahá'u'lláh's daughter, Bahíyyih Khánum, understood this.

When Bahíyyih Khánum was young and living in Persia, her Father was put in prison because of His religious beliefs. No matter how hard life was, Bahíyyih Khánum and her family followed and served Him. When Bahá'u'lláh died, Bahíyyih Khánum did all she could to help 'Abdu'l-Bahá. When 'Abdu'l-Bahá died, she looked after Shoghi Effendi. They often called her by the title Bahá'u'lláh gave her, the Greatest Holy Leaf.

The Greatest Holy Leaf didn't just look after her Family—or even just the Bahá'ís. She knew that Bahá'u'lláh wanted her to think of everyone as one family.

Once some Bahá'ís traveled many hundreds of miles to the Holy Land. The Muslim wife of one of the Bahá'ís went, too. Even though they traveled by car, crossing the Syrian Desert took days. Everyone was tired and grumpy, and some of them were rude to the woman. She felt sad but said nothing.

Finally they reached 'Abdu'l-Bahá's house. The women were eager to visit Bahá'u'lláh's daughter. They found her waiting outside to greet them, but she did not lead them right in. She was waiting for someone else.

Nervously, the Muslim woman stepped forward. Bahíyyih Khánum hugged her, took her hand, and led them all inside. She seated the Muslim woman beside her, and she gave her own ring to her special guest.

The woman never forgot Bahíyyih Khánum's kindness.

And the Bahá'ís never forgot their lesson: We are all one family. ★

O CHILDREN OF MEN!
Know ye not why We created you all from the same dust?
That no one should exalt himself over the other.
Ponder at all times in your hearts how ye were created.
Since We have created you all from one same substance
it is incumbent on you to be even as one soul,
to walk with the same feet, eat with the same mouth
and dwell in the same land, that from your inmost being,
by your deeds and actions, the signs of oneness
and the essence of detachment may be made manifest.
Such is My counsel to you, O concourse of light!
Heed ye this counsel that ye may obtain the fruit
of holiness from the tree of wondrous glory.

— Bahá'u'lláh, Hidden Words, Arabic No. 68

Illustrated by Carrie Kneisler

Thank You, Isfandíyár

Written by Rick Johnson
Illustrated by Keith Kresge

When I was growing up, Halloween* was a great time, even for a kid in a wheelchair. I was actually famous in my neighborhood because I had the coolest homemade Halloween costumes—like one time I was a haunted semi-truck rolling along with headlights flashing wildly and scary sounds playing. Another year I was a soda machine that dispensed real (empty) soda cans! I think my favorite costume was when I was a washing machine and Dad recorded sounds of the big laundry downtown and I played those and flipped my lid. My most memorable Halloween, though, was the year I was a witch with long rubber worms for hair. It wasn't so much the costume—but that year was especially memorable because I met Isfandíyár.

*Halloween, the evening of October 31, is a day on which many children in North America, and some other regions, wear costumes and visit houses door-to-door, saying "trick or treat," and receive candy.

Bahá'u'lláh: Principles Related to the Oneness of God and the Oneness of Humanity

Isfandíyár—yes, that was his amazing name—was my first real friend, and he truly changed my life. But, I should slow down with the story because I'm getting ahead of myself.

In our neighborhood, I knew most of the people, and everything was fine. So, most years, I'd go out by myself and I'd roll up to the door or porch and shout "TRICK OR TREAT!" like any other kid. But the really memorable year, things didn't go exactly like always. That year, I ran into some bullies stealing candy bags away from other kids. There were three of them, and they just stepped out of the dark when I was alone.

"Well, lookie here—a witch in a wheelchair! Ooooh, I am soooo scared."

"Hey, witchie, if you're so powerful, why don't you heal yourself?"

"Yeah, you must be a fake witch . . . let's see if you can stop me from taking your candy!"

I was just starting to feel really scared when another voice yelled, "Leave him alone!" It sounded loud enough to hear across town, and those guys froze! "Leave him alone! Now!" The voice really wasn't so much loud as determined and commanding. These cowardly bullies were not of a mind to argue even though this new person did not look bigger or older. Something in his voice and look just made you want to say, "Yes, sir!"

The bullies moved off, and I looked at this new person. I didn't know his name, but I recognized him from school. "Thanks, I really appreciate what you did."

"No way I was going to let those guys get away with that," he replied. "My parents taught me to take care of people. I'm new here—who's got the best treats?"

"The next house is Gorman's, and they do homemade candy apples . . . Come on, let's go!"

104 Bahá'u'lláh: Principles Related to the Oneness of God and the Oneness of Humanity

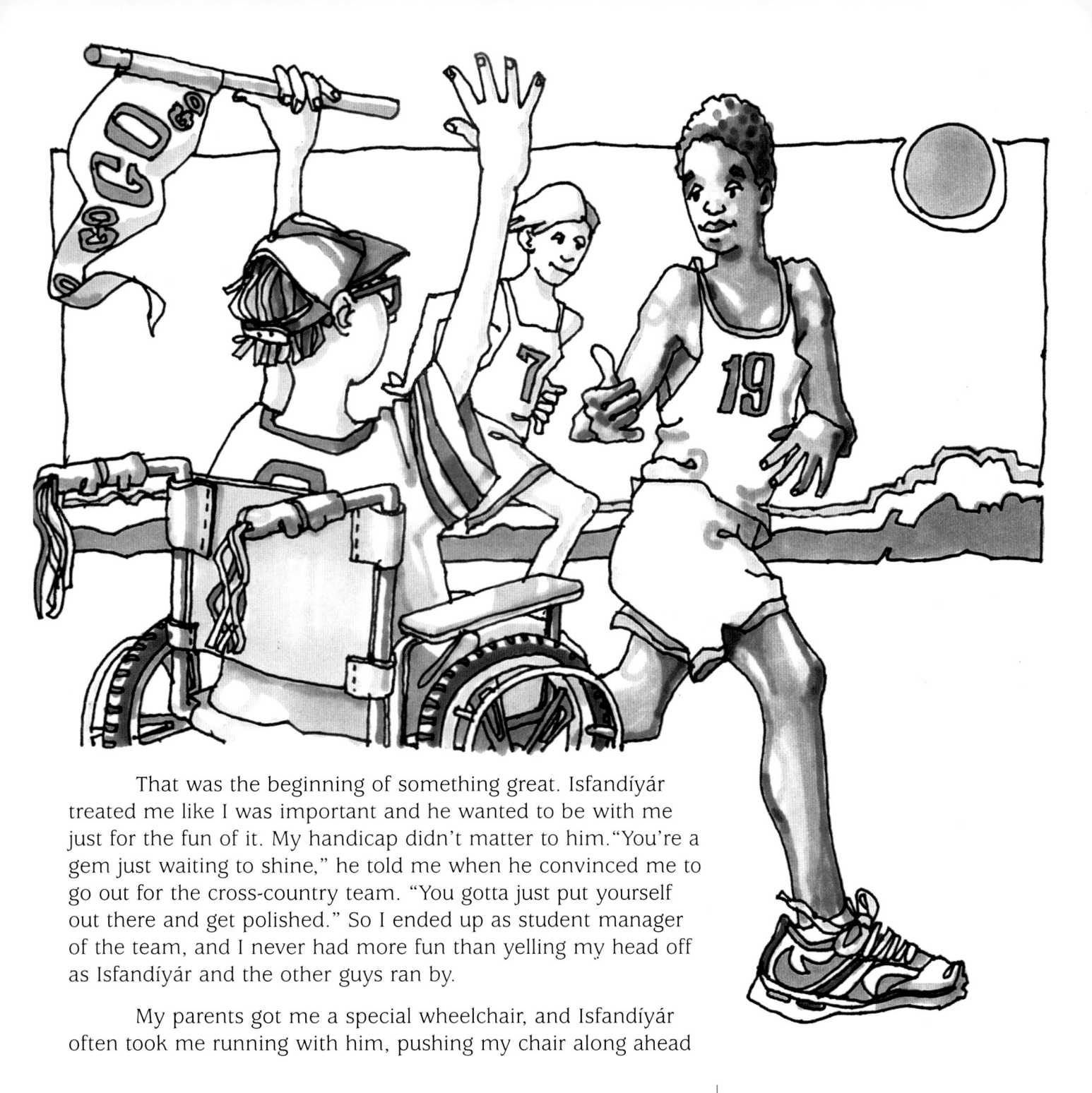

That was the beginning of something great. Isfandíyár treated me like I was important and he wanted to be with me just for the fun of it. My handicap didn't matter to him. "You're a gem just waiting to shine," he told me when he convinced me to go out for the cross-country team. "You gotta just put yourself out there and get polished." So I ended up as student manager of the team, and I never had more fun than yelling my head off as Isfandíyár and the other guys ran by.

My parents got me a special wheelchair, and Isfandíyár often took me running with him, pushing my chair along ahead of him or urging me as I learned to roll along at a pretty good clip myself. He was a truly devoted friend. Some people teased me or ignored me because of my handicap, but not Isfandíyár. He liked the goofy card tricks I showed him, and he taught me to blow a few notes on his tuba.

One time he wrote a poem for English class that was called "Friends," and that pretty well summed it up. We were friends no matter what. He saved me in chemistry class once by running back to school in the rain to get my chem notes. Without those notes, I'd have bombed a big test. That was just the way it was with Isfandíyár. When he won the state cross-country title, the first thing he did after finishing was to find me and give me a high five, and that was the picture that showed up on sports pages across the state.

Even now, twenty-five years later, I still look at the yellowed newspaper often and think of what Isfandíyár's friendship meant to me. He's never changed, even now that he is president of a famous medical school.

Isfandíyár was the first Bahá'í I ever knew, and he told me one day, as we sat in the shade after running, that his namesake was a hero of the Bahá'í Faith. "I'm named after an incredibly courageous Ethiopian who served in the household of Bahá'u'lláh, the Founder of the Bahá'í Faith," he said, "and I think he is one of the great heroes of my Faith."

"When Bahá'u'lláh was imprisoned during some horrible persecutions of the Bahá'ís, His family was left with no one to take care of them. Enemies were looking for Isfandíyár in order to force him to betray other Bahá'ís. But despite the danger, he returned to the looted ruins of Bahá'u'lláh's house looking for Bahá'u'lláh's Family. 'Where are the children?' he asked. 'What has happened to their mother?' Through courageous, devoted searching, he was reunited with the family. Bahá'u'lláh's family was homeless and had no money or friends. Although a hundred police wanted to capture, torture, and kill him, Isfandíyár refused to hide and went boldly around the city attending to the family's needs and paying off debts left in Bahá'u'lláh's name after His imprisonment. He could not bear to see the family suffer or the good name of Bahá'u'lláh dishonored. Even when other unfaithful family members and servants fled, Isfandiíyár remained loyal to Bahá'u'lláh."

"I can see some of those qualities in you, too," I said.

Bahá'u'lláh: Principles Related to the Oneness of God and the Oneness of Humanity | 107

"I'm really proud of my name," he replied, "Isfandíyár loved the truth so much that nothing scared him. That's the way I want to be."

Even now, years later, I can see Isfandíyár sitting there under the tree, smiling as he talked. He made the most difficult things seem so natural that you just wanted to do them. It made me happy just to be around him.

"My mother made some needlework for me," Isfandíyár continued. "She put some words about Isfandíyár into needlepoint and framed it for me. They're words of 'Abdu'l-Bahá, the Son of Bahá'u'lláh: 'If a perfect man could be found in the world, that man was Isfandíyár . . . Whenever I think of Isfandíyár, I am moved to tears, although he passed away fifty years ago.'"

I saw that needlework many times as Isfandíyár and I went through high school together. It hung in his room over his bed, and those words just seemed to soak into him. It was wonderful to see how he strived to love and care about others as the earlier Isfandíyár had done.

I am now over forty years old myself and see my old friend only rarely, but I think of him often. He made doing new or difficult things seem natural. He made me feel like I could do things I never dreamed were in me. I guess that's why I just finished "running" my nineteenth marathon in my wheelchair and why I love Bahá'u'lláh so very much. Thank you, Isfandíyár, my noble friend. ★

Appendix

Questions for Reflection and Discussion

Prayers and Meditations of Bahá'u'lláh

1. Reflect on your own life: What is your own experience with prayer? What is prayer?
2. Why should we pray?
3. When should we pray?
4. How should we pray?
5. How do we know our prayers are answered?
6. How do the stories "Saving the Silver-Tongued Nightingale," "A Prayer for Mírzá Ja'far," and "The Tree of Life" each illustrate the importance of prayer?

Loving Acts of Bahá'u'lláh

1. In the stories "Father of the Poor," "One Meritorious Act," and "The Friend at the Crossroads" how does Bahá'u'lláh show His love for others?
2. Read again the quotations on pages 18 and 26. How do these quotations help us understand the meaning of love?
3. What are some of the ways that we know that Bahá'u'lláh loves us?
4. What are some ways that we can show our love for Bahá'u'lláh?
5. How can our love for Bahá'u'lláh help us become more loving to others?
6. What are some practical ways that we can show our love to our parents, our brothers and sisters, our teachers, and our friends?

Bahá'u'lláh and the Children of His Household

1. There are many little stories about Bahá'u'lláh that are retold in the stories "Summertime," "The Prison and the Garden," and "The Power of Love." What are some of the ways that Bahá'u'lláh shows His love for children in these stories?
2. Why do you think that Bahá'u'lláh took the time to show His love for children? Why do you think that children are important members of every community?

3. What do you think that Bahá'u'lláh means when He says, "He that bringeth up his son or the son of another, it is as though he hath brought up a son of Mine"?
4. How do we know that Bahá'u'lláh loves all children, not just some?
5. What do you imagine it would be like to grow up in the Household of Bahá'u'lláh?

The Station of Bahá'u'lláh as Stated by 'Abdu'l-Bahá

1. Why do you think 'Abdu'l-Bahá says, "Verily, ye are the proofs of Bahá'u'lláh"? How is it that our lives can be a proof of the power of Bahá'u'lláh?
2. Why do you think it was not possible for the unjust king to keep Bahá'u'lláh imprisoned forever?
3. How do 'Abdu'l-Bahá's actions show His love for Bahá'u'lláh?
4. Why is it important for us to know the ways that 'Abdu'l-Bahá recognized Bahá'u'lláh and showed His love through service?
5. What are some of the ways that we can be like 'Abdu'l-Bahá and show our love for Bahá'u'lláh?

The Childhood of Bahá'u'lláh

1. When and where was Bahá'u'lláh born? Who were His parents?
2. Why do we celebrate His Birthday as a Holy Day? What are some of the ways that you celebrate this important Holy Day in your family and in your community?
3. In the story "Bahá'u'lláh's Fishes," how does Ellie learn that Bahá'u'lláh will protect her sister while on her Youth Year of Service?
4. How does the story "The Puppet Show," let us know that Bahá'u'lláh showed great wisdom while He was still a child?
5. What could you tell your friends about the birth of Bahá'u'lláh? What could you tell them about Bahá'u'lláh's childhood?

The Youth and Early Manhood of Bahá'u'lláh

1. What actions did Bahá'u'lláh take to protect His father and Ṭáhirih when they were in trouble?
2. What spiritual qualities does Bahá'u'lláh show in the stories "The Badasht Conference," "Lives of Service," and "Escape to Ṭihrán"?
3. How can we show those same spiritual qualities in our own lives?
4. How did Bahá'u'lláh promote the Cause of the Báb during the Conference of Badasht?

5. As a young man, Bahá'u'lláh had many dramatic episodes while promoting the Cause of the Báb. Why do you think He was such an active Bábí during those years?
6. What are some of the powerful actions that we can take while we are young?

Principles Related to the Oneness of God and the Oneness of Humanity

1. What does Bahá'u'lláh mean when He says, "Ye are the fruits of one tree, and the leaves of one branch"?
2. How do the stories "Isfandíyár," "A Journey across a Desert," and "Thank You, Isfandíyár" demonstrate the principle of the oneness of humanity?
3. What are some of the differences and what are some of the similarities of all the people you know?
4. How do our differences help us? How do our similarities help us?
5. What would the world be like if everyone understood the principles of the oneness of God and the oneness of humanity?
6. How can we help all our friends learn about and understand Bahá'u'lláh's beautiful principle of oneness?

Glossary

'Abdu'l-Bahá: (ab-dol ba-ha) "Servant of Bahá." Bahá'u'lláh's eldest Son and the first to believe in Him. He was appointed by Bahá'u'lláh in His Will and Testament to be His successor and the Center of His Covenant. Also known as the Most Great Branch.

'Akká: (ack-caw) An ancient city north of Mount Carmel in present-day Israel where Bahá'u'lláh spent the last twenty-four years of His life.

Allegiance: Loyalty, or the obligation of loyalty, as to a nation, ruler or cause.

Apostasy: To abandon one's beliefs.

Ásíyih Khánum: (aw-see-eh khaw-noom) The wife of Bahá'u'lláh and the mother of 'Abdu'l-Bahá, Bahíyyih Khánum, and Mírzá Mihdí. She was surnamed "Navváb" (meaning "Highness") by Bahá'u'lláh, and He paid her a tribute by naming her His "perpetual consort in all the worlds of God."

Assemblage: A group of people gathered together for a common purpose.

Báb, The: (bob) "Gate." The title taken by Mírzá 'Alí-Muhammad (1819–50), the Forerunner of Bahá'u'lláh. A young merchant from Shíráz, He declared His mission in 1844 and was executed in 1850.

Bábí: (bob-ee) A follower of the Báb; of, or pertaining to the religion of the Báb.

Badasht: (ba-dasht) A small village in Mázindarán where Bahá'u'lláh conducted a conference lasting twenty-two days, in June–July 1848, to proclaim the independence of the Bábí Faith from Islám, thus making clear that a new Dispensation in religion had begun.

Baghdád: (bag-dawd) The capital city of 'Iráq, to which Bahá'u'lláh was exiled in 1853. He lived there, except for a period of two years, until His further exile in 1863, recreating the Bábí community and revealing some of His most important Writings. He called Baghdád the "City of God."

Bahá: (ba-ha) "Glory" or "Splendor." An Arabic word with the numerical value of nine, which is referred to in many prophecies of this Day. It is the title of Bahá'u'lláh and the root word of the Greatest Name, "Alláh-u-Abhá."

Bahá'í: (ba-ha-ee) A follower of Bahá'u'lláh; of, or pertaining to, the Bahá'í Faith.

Bahá'u'lláh: (ba-ha-ol-lah) "The Glory of God." A title of Mírzá Husayn-'Alí (1817–92), the One designated by the Báb as "Him Whom God shall make manifest."

Bahíyyih Khánum: (ba-hee-eh khaw-noom) The devoted daughter of Bahá'u'lláh, entitled by Him the "Greatest Holy Leaf." Her entire life was spent assisting those around her—Bahá'u'lláh, 'Abdu'l-Bahá, and later the Guardian, Shoghi Effendi. Bahá'u'lláh wrote that she attained "a station such as none other woman hath surpassed."

Bahjí: (bah-jee) "Delight." Originally, the name given to a beautiful garden north of 'Akká. The name is now used to designate the mansion nearby, where Bahá'u'lláh lived from 1879 until His ascension in 1892. His shrine is adjacent to the mansion. Built by 'Údí Khammár for his own residence, after his death it was rented by 'Abdu'l-Bahá for a meager sum when it was abandoned during an epidemic. Later it was purchased and is now a place of pilgrimage for Bahá'ís.

Calligraphy: Beautiful penmanship, which, in Persian and Arabic writing, is treated as an art and is considered indicative of the writer's education and social status.

Chádor: (cha-door) A black cloth worn by Iranian women, required by law, which covers their hair and their bodies.

Constantinople: The former name for Istanbul, where Bahá'u'lláh was exiled in 1863, and where Bahá'u'lláh initiated the first phase of His proclamation to the kings and rulers of the world.

Haifa: A modern city at the foot of Mount Carmel, across the bay from 'Akká.

Imám: (eh-mawm) One of the twelve hereditary successors of the Prophet Muḥammad, according to Shí'ih Muslim belief. In Islám, the term also refers to the religious leader who leads the prayers in a mosque.

Írán: (ee-rawn) The country formerly called Persia, where the Báb and Bahá'u'lláh were born.

Islám: (ess-lawm) The religion of Muḥammad.

Kad-Khudá: (kad kho-da) Chief of a ward or parish in a town; headman of a village.

Letters of the Living: The first eighteen disciples of the Báb.

Long Obligatory Prayer: One of three obligatory prayers. Bahá'ís must choose one of these prayers to recite each day.

Martyr: One who willingly gives up his life rather than renounce his religious beliefs.

Mazra'ih: (moz-ra-eh) "Farm" or "field"; refers to the house about seven kilometers north of 'Akká where Bahá'u'lláh lived immediately after leaving the confines of the city of 'Akká in 1877. He stayed there for about two years.

Mírzá 'Alí-Muḥammad: (meer-zaw a-lee mo-ham-mad) See **Báb, The**.

Mírzá Buzurg: (meer-zaw bo-zorg) The father of Bahá'u'lláh, also called Mírzá 'Abbás.

Mírzá Ḥusayn-'Alí: (meer-zaw ho-sain a-lee) The given name of Bahá'u'lláh.

Mount Carmel: A mountain in Israel long regarded as a holy place by Egyptians, Jews, and Christians alike. The mountain ends abruptly at the sea at Haifa. The Shrine of the Báb as well as the Bahá'í World Center are located on the mountain overlooking the center of Haifa and the bay beyond.

Muḥammad: (mo-ham-mad) The Prophet or Manifestation of God (A.D. 570–632) Who founded the religion of Islám and revealed the Qur'án. His name means "highly praised." His followers are known as Muslims.

Muslim: (muss-lem) A follower of Islám, the religion of Muḥammad.

Palestine: The land between the Mediterranean Sea and the Jordan River that was occupied by the Hebrews in the second millennium B.C. and was the scene of most of the events described in the Bible. In modern times this country, formerly a province of the Ottoman Empire, and then a British-mandated territory, was divided between Israel, Jordan, and Egypt in 1948. Bahá'u'lláh lived the last twenty-four years of His life in Palestine.

Panoply: The complete arms and armor of a warrior.

Pilgrimage: A journey to a shrine or other holy place; in general terms, a long search that has moral implications.

Qazvín: (gaz-veen) A city in Írán, one hundred miles northwest of Ṭihrán, where Ṭáhirih was born.

Quddús: (god-doos) The Letter of the Living who was first in rank among the Letters. He accompanied the Báb on pilgrimage to Mecca and led the Bábís in defending themselves at Shaykh Ṭabarsí. He was martyred in his native town of Bárfurúsh (known today as Bábul).

Qur'án: (gore-awn) The Holy Book of Islám, revealed by Muḥammad during His ministry of twenty-two years (A.D. 610–32). It is divided into súrihs, or chapters.

Qurratu'l-'Ayn: (gore-ra-tal-ain) see **Ṭáhirih**.

Ramaḍan: The ninth month in the Islamic calendar, during which Muslims fast from dawn to dusk.

Revelation: A term sometimes referring to the entire body of teachings of a Manifestation and sometimes designating the process by which He receives and spontaneously transmits the Word of God to humanity.

Riḍván: (rez-vawn) "Paradise." A name given to two gardens visited by Bahá'u'lláh. The first was the garden outside Baghdád where Bahá'u'lláh revealed to His followers in 1863 that He was the Promised One foretold by the Báb; the second is the garden outside 'Akká which He frequently visited during the last period of His life. The term also designates the most important festival of the Bahá'í calendar, the commemoration of the twelve days in 1863 when Bahá'u'lláh announced His station.

Rúḥu'lláh: (roh-ho-la) The son of Varqá, who saved his father's life by his recitation of Bahá'u'lláh's Long Obligatory Prayer.

Scripture: A sacred writing or book, or a passage from such a writing or book.

Shaykh Aḥmad-i-Aḥsá'í: (shake ah-mad eh ah-saw-ee) The first of two heralds of the Báb. Born in 1753, he spent the last forty years of his life teaching about the imminent advent of the Qá'im. He died in 1826.

Shoghi Effendi: 'Abdu'l-Bahá's eldest grandson, whom He appointed as Guardian of the Bahá'í Faith in His Will and Testament. He was born in 1897 and served as the Guardian from his appointment in 1921 until his death in 1957.

Siyyid Káẓim-i-Rashtí: (sey-yed kaw-zim eh rash-tee) With Shaykh Aḥmad, he was one of the two heralds of the Báb. It was from him that Mullá Ḥusayn received his inspiration to go in search of the Qá'im.

Ṭáhirih: (taw-her-eh) "The Pure One"; a title given by Bahá'u'lláh to the only female Letter of the Living. A figure of great importance in the Bábí Faith, Ṭáhirih was born about 1817–18 and was martyred in 1852.

Ṭihrán: (teh-rawn) The birthplace of Bahá'u'lláh, the capital of Írán, and the place where Bahá'u'lláh lived and later was imprisoned until His exile in 1853.

Varqá: (var-gaw) A follower of the Báb who was a poet, writer, and intellectual.

Bibliography

1. Saving the Silver-Tongued Nightingale © 2001 Jean Gould
Balyuzi, H. M. *Eminent Bahá'ís in the Time of Bahá'u'lláh*, 76–83. Oxford: George Ronald, 1985.

2. A Prayer for Mirza Ja'far © 2001 Gail Radley
'Abdu'l-Bahá. *Memorials of the Faithful*, 156–58. Translated and annotated by Marzieh Gail. Wilmette, Ill.: Bahá'í Publishing Trust, 1971.

3. Tree of Life © 2001 William Rick Johnson
Blomfield, Lady Sara. *The Chosen Highway*, 39–69. Wilmette, Ill.: Bahá'í Publishing Trust, 1940.

4. Father of the Poor © 2001 Gail Radley
Ruhe, David. *Robe of Light*, 39–53. Oxford: George Ronald, 1994.

5. One Meritorious Act © 2001 Susan Nadimi
Nabíl-i-A'ẓam (Mullá Muḥammad-i-Zarandí). *The Dawn-Breakers: Nabíl's Narrative of the Early Days of the Bahá'í Revelation*, 607–608. Translated and edited by Shoghi Effendi. New York: Bahá'í Publishing Committee, 1932. Shoghi Effendi. *God Passes By*, 71. Wilmette, Ill.: Bahá'í Publishing Trust, 1944.

6. The Friend at the Crossroads © 2001 Sally Cordova
Balyuzi, H. M. *Bahá'u'lláh: The King of Glory*, 151. Oxford: George Ronald, 1980.

7. Summertime © 2001 Alexander Haskell
Blomfield, Lady Sara. *The Chosen Highway*, 97–98. Wilmette, Ill.: Bahá'í Publishing Trust, 1940.

8. The Prison and the Garden © 2001 Susan Nadimi
Shoghi Effendi. *God Passes By*, 179, 183–220. Wilmette, Ill.: Bahá'í Publishing Trust, 1944.

9. The Power of Love © 2001 William Rick Johnson
Blomfield, Lady Sara. *The Chosen Highway*, 39–69. Wilmette, Ill.: Bahá'í Publishing Trust, 1940. 'Abdu'l-Bahá. *Memorials of the Faithful*, 26–28. Translated and annotated by Marzieh Gail. Wilmette, Ill.: Bahá'í Publishing Trust, 1971.

10. The Prisoner with Power © 2001 William Rick Johnson
'Abdu'l-Bahá. *Memorials of the Faithful*, 26–28. Translated and annotated by Marzieh Gail. Wilmette, Ill.: Bahá'í Publishing Trust, 1971.

11. The Truth of Bahá'u'lláh's Mission © 2001 William Rick Johnson
'Abdu'l-Bahá. *The Promulgation of Universal Peace*, 461–462. Wilmette, Ill.: Bahá'í Publishing Trust, 1982.

12. The Greatest Father-Son Story of All Time © 2001 William Rick Johnson
Taherzadeh, Adib. *The Covenant of Bahá'u'lláh*, 190–191. Oxford: George Ronald, 1992. Annamarie Honnold, ed., comp., *Vignettes from the Life of 'Abdu'l-Bahá*, 146–147. Oxford: George Ronald, 1982.

13. Bahá'u'lláh's Fishes © 2001 William Rick Johnson
Nabíl-i-A'zam (Mullá Muḥammad-i-Zarandí). *The Dawn-Breakers: Nabíl's Narrative of the Early Days of the Bahá'í Revelation*, 119–20. Translated and edited by Shoghi Effendi. New York: Bahá'í Publishing Committee, 1932.

14. Bahá'u'lláh Is Born © 2001 Susan Nadimi
Nabíl-i-A'zam (Mullá Muḥammad-i-Zarandí). *The Dawn-Breakers: Nabíl's Narrative of the Early Days of the Bahá'í Revelation*, 12–13. Translated and edited by Shoghi Effendi. New York: Bahá'í Publishing Committee, 1932.

15. The Puppet Show © 2001 Susan Nadimi
Ruhe, David. *Robe of Light*, 24–35, 39, 41. Oxford: George Ronald, 1994.

16. The Badasht Conference © 2001 Lily Ayman
Nabíl-i-A'zam (Mullá Muḥammad-i-Zarandí). *The Dawn-Breakers: Nabíl's Narrative of the Early Days of the Bahá'í Revelation*, 288–300. Translated and edited by Shoghi Effendi. New York: Bahá'í Publishing Committee, 1932. Shoghi Effendi. *God Passes By*, 31–33. Wilmette, Ill.: Bahá'í Publishing Trust, 1944.

17. Lives of Service © 2001 Gail Radley
Ruhe, David. *Robe of Light*, 41–48. Oxford: George Ronald, 1994.

18. Escape to Ṭihrán © 2001 Jean Gould
Nabíl-i-A'zam (Mullá Muḥammad-i-Zarandí). *The Dawn-Breakers: Nabíl's Narrative of the Early Days of the Bahá'í Revelation*, 283–87. Translated and edited by Shoghi Effendi. New York: Bahá'í Publishing Committee, 1932.

19. Isfandíyár © 2001 Patti Rae Tomarelli
'Abdu'l-Bahá. *The Promulgation of Universal Peace*, 421–23. Wilmette, Ill.: Bahá'í Publishing Trust, 1982.

20. Journey across a Desert © 2001 Gail Radley
Faizi, A. Q. *A Gift of Love: Offered to the Greatest Holy Leaf*, 21–26. Compiled and edited by Gloria Faizi. 1982.

21. Thank You, Isfandíyár © 2001 William Rick Johnson
'Abdu'l-Bahá. *The Promulgation of Universal Peace*, 421–23. Wilmette, Ill.: Bahá'í Publishing Trust, 1982. Faizi, A. Q. *A Gift of Love: Offered to the Greatest Holy Leaf*, 21–26. Compiled and edited by Gloria Faizi. 1982.

Index

'Abdu'l-Bahá, 9, 15, 16, 21, 46, 50, 51, 55, 58, 59, 60, 61, 62, 98, 99, 103, 104, 111
Abhá, 87
Ablution, 7
Africa, 65, 66, 69
Allegiance, 4
Áqá 'Abdu's-Ṣaliḥ, 42, 43
Ásíyih Khánum, 20

Báb, The, 80, 84, 88, 89
Bábí, 6, 23, 24, 80, 81, 84
Badasht, 79
Baghdád, 27, 29
Bahá'í, 4, 5, 41, 46, 49, 65, 74, 76, 77, 110
Bahá'u'lláh, 3, 4, 5, 6, 7, 8, 9, 13, 14, 15, 16, 19, 21, 25, 29, 35, 36, 37, 38, 39, 43, 45, 46, 50, 51, 52, 53, 54, 55, 60, 61, 62, 65, 67, 68, 69, 71, 73, 74, 75, 76, 77, 80, 81, 82, 84, 85, 86, 88, 90, 92, 95, 98, 99, 100, 101, 102, 103, 104, 110, 111
Bahíyyih Khánum, 15, 16, 45, 103, 104
Bahjí, 52
Brave, 72, 83

Candle, 72
Children, 15, 16, 20, 27, 39, 41, 42, 45, 46, 65, 90, 110, 111
Comfort, 20, 85
Constantinople, 29
Courage, 19
Courtesy, 15

Dispensation, 84

Education, 46
Effulgence, 87

Family, 4, 13, 14, 15, 19, 39, 44, 46, 86, 98, 103, 104, 110
Father of the Poor, 19, 20, 21, 90, 95
Fearless, 92
Feast, 21
Friend, 27, 28, 37, 58, 65, 94, 107, 109, 111

Garden, 8, 35, 36, 39, 52, 56, 60, 62, 82, 95
Generous, 20, 26
Gift, 6, 21
Glory, 6, 24, 40, 72, 76, 81, 84
Guardian, 16
Guest, 104

Haifa, 52
Heal, 107
Health, 23
Heart, 4, 16, 20, 25, 36, 49, 51, 53, 59, 71, 98
Heaven, 32
Help, 5, 9, 20, 24, 43, 44, 46, 53, 59, 65, 67, 68, 75, 85, 86, 90, 94, 103
Hero, 110
History, 3, 56
Honor, 83

Imám, 25
Isfandíyár, 98, 99, 100, 101, 102, 106, 108, 109, 110, 111
Islam, 81, 82, 84

Jail, 56
Justice, 79

Kad-khudá, 90, 92
Khatúm-Ján, 94
Kindness, 15, 55, 104

Light, 43, 72, 94, 102
Long Obligatory Prayer, 7
Love, 11, 14, 15, 16, 18, 22, 28, 29, 32, 36, 37, 41, 42, 43, 44, 45, 46, 52, 55, 59, 61, 62, 69, 71, 84, 102, 111

Mercy, 40, 90
Meritorious, 25
Miracles, 56
Mírzá Buzurg, 19, 67, 85, 86
Mission, 54
Modesty, 83
Moses, 36
Mosque, 23, 89
Mother of Consolation, 20, 95
Mount Carmel, 52
Muḥammad, 4, 24, 36
Muḥammad-Hádí, 92, 94
Mullá Taqí, 88, 89, 90
Muslim, 3, 4, 23, 84, 88, 90, 94, 104

Neighbor, 26
Noble, 111

Oneness, 105

Palestine, 61
Panoply, 56
Pilgrimage, 16
Plant, 35, 59
Power, 13, 20, 41, 44, 45, 49, 56, 68, 76, 84, 85, 92
Prayer, 6, 7, 8, 9, 10, 13, 15, 23, 89
Prison, 8, 38, 39, 50, 51, 52, 56, 99, 103
Proof, 6, 45, 48, 55
Prophet, 24, 50
Protect, 21
Puppet, 74, 76
Pure, 81, 84, 89, 92, 94, 95, 98
Purity, 83

Qazvín, 88, 92, 94
Quddús, 80, 81, 82

Ramaḍan, 87
Religion, 45
Respect, 14, 15, 45, 46, 52, 95
Revelation, 81
Rich, 26, 90
Riḍván, 35, 39
Roses, 37

School, 13, 42, 44, 46, 54, 57, 67, 107, 109, 111
Science, 13
Scriptures, 3
Service, 45, 62, 65, 66, 85
Sháhzádih Gate, 94
Shoghi Effendi, 103
Soldiers, 74, 76
Soul, 30, 72
Strength, 45
Summer, 11, 12, 33, 37, 80

Tablet, 81, 84
Ṭáhirih, 81, 82, 83, 84, 88, 89, 92, 94, 95
Teachings, 52, 55, 81
Tears, 15, 25, 111
Thank, 37, 106, 111
Ṭihrán, 88, 90
Tree of Life, 11, 16
Trust, 26
Truth, 4, 54, 55, 79, 90, 92, 111

Unity, 44, 97

Varqá, 3, 4, 5, 6, 7
Veil, 72, 82, 83

Water of Life, 14, 16
Wealth, 20

Yazd, 3
Youth, 41, 43

Bahá'u'lláh's Exiles

November 12	1817	Birth of Bahá'u'lláh in Ṭihrán, Iran
October	1835	Marriage of Bahá'u'lláh to Ásíyih Khánum, known as Navváb
August 15	1852	Attempt on the life of Náṣiri'd-Dín Sháh, after which Bahá'u'lláh was imprisoned in the Síyáh-Chál
December	1852	Bahá'u'lláh is released from the Síyáh-Chál
January 12	1853	Bahá'u'lláh is banished to Baghdád
April 8	1853	Bahá'u'lláh arrives in Baghdád
April 21–May 1	1863	Bahá'u'lláh announces that He is the Promised One in the Garden of Riḍván
August 16	1863	Bahá'u'lláh arrives in Constantinople
December 12	1863	Bahá'u'lláh arrives in Adrianople
August 31	1863	Bahá'u'lláh arrives in 'Akká
June	1877	Bahá'u'lláh leaves 'Akká for Mazra'ih
September	1879	Bahá'u'lláh begins His residence at Bahjí
May 29	1892	Ascension of Bahá'u'lláh at Bahjí